A BOOK OF DESIRE

NOTES OF A PSYCHOLOGIST

Dr Lia T. Asandei

Grosvenor House
Publishing Limited

This book is published by
Grosvenor House Publishing Ltd
Link House
140 The Broadway, Tolworth, Surrey, KT6 7HT.
www.grosvenorhousepublishing.co.uk

A CIP record for this book
is available from the British Library

ISBN 978-1-83975-393-0

Dr Lia T. Asandei, 2019

To my father

Wish I was afraid of fire
But instead, I live off it
I fall for it. I beg for it
I cannot breathe without it
I cannot forget without it.
It's strange I should love rain.
I am fire from fire
Burning myself down
Until all is melting ash.

From *Journal of a Melancholic,* unpublished

PREFACE

In his book *Beyond Good and Evil*, the philosopher and poet Friedrich Nietzsche writes that, 'It is possible that under the holy story and distortion of the life of Jesus there is hidden one of the most painful cases of the martyrdom of *knowledge about love*: the martyrdom of the most innocent and most craving heart, that never had enough of any human love, that *demanded* love, that demanded inexorably and frantically to be loved and nothing else, with terrible fights against those who refused him their love; the story of a poor soul insatiated and insatiable in love, that had to invent hell to send thither those who *would not* love him – and that at last, enlightened about human love, had to invent a God who is entire love, entire *capacity* for love...'

In the past sixteen years I worked as a therapist and clinical psychologist for NHS Mental Health Services (South London and

Maudsley NHS Foundation Trust, North East London NHS Foundation Trust and Whittington Health NHS Trust). I have always been touched to discover that my patients too, are insatiable in love, that they desire and need to be loved. I am impossibly touched when sometimes they say in sessions that they never told anyone before about something terribly important that had happened in their life.

In our work together we always talk about love, desire, loss, angst, pain; we work at the junction of Psychoanalysis and Philosophy.

I believe that my analysands continue to search for love even in therapy.

I always hope that they will come to love their life.

But in all my work I came to realise that I love their lives too, and that is why their stories (with their accord) had to be told, and this book had to be written.

London, August 2020

CONTENTS

I. WORDS OF LOVE

The ravaging light
of full moon nights
Has torn my flesh into a thousand silent signs
Stars and wolves have gathered them
And put them into words.
I have tried and tried
But I could not read them.
You are reading them to me
And I listen to your words
Again and again.

From *Journal of a Melancholic*, unpublished

In psychoanalytic theory, the famous French psychoanalyst and psychiatrist Jacques Lacan teaches that love is a form of suicide.

We are reminded that love changes us, that love changes things in our lives; it changes our lives. For lots of us, love is an endgame, even though we do not necessarily recognise it as such.

There are patients who had started, unconsciously, to behave in a certain way in relationships, because of an earlier relationship that ended badly. And how can a relationship end if not badly? It either ends badly or it never ends. Should we aim to shake hands and pat our shoulders when we break apart?

Even if we do so, there is regret, bitterness, sorrow, confusion, anger. It would be quite difficult to part as friends, although not impossible. Perhaps being friends afterwards is another symptom, it says something about us, but what? That we do not care any longer, that we still want to keep the person in our life, that we still need them, that we try to use them. It will mean different things for different people.

Religion teaches us that in the beginning was the Word.

In his Seminar on Transference, Jacques Lacan states that, 'in the beginning there was love'. He refers to the beginning of psychoanalysis, the 'talking cure', and its first patient, Anna O.

Anna O. was at the centre of Sigmund Freud's (father of Psychoanalysis) original treatment of hysteria. Her first doctor mentions her saying words to herself, which sounded like 'melancholic phantasies which held poetic beauty'. Melancholia and poetry are part of the beginning of Psychoanalysis.

Anna O. fell in love with her doctor, Joseph Breuer; Jacques Lacan notices that whether the doctor responded to her request for love or not, it did not matter all the same.

This sort of love came to be considered in psychological practice as *transference*, an interpersonal phenomenon where a person appears to redirect to specific people feelings meant for others, feelings meant for certain other significant people in their lives. This transfer of love may happen in various life situations, but it is very likely to occur in a therapy situation. Both love and hatred can be transferred.

Psychoanalysis reminds us how important words are, for both love and hate.

Indeed, they seem to follow a common path with our destiny.

Besides words, we also have feelings, and actions, and memories, but what would they be without expression, words and meaning?

Jacques Lacan goes as far as to say that, 'our unconscious life is structured as a language'. We seem to place irrevocable heaviness on words and what they mean for our psychical life. Our deepest layer of mind is bound intimately to the language and the ideas that have accompanied us from the start of life.

Recently, Andrew D. (all real names have been changed in the book), a patient in his late fifties who worked in a military administration department, told me that he had an incident at work that lead to him taking a long absence of sickness related to anxiety and depression. He described his work at the Ministry of Defence as highly important and very much dictated by rules and protocols.

A new female colleague of similar age, with a senior administrative role, had joined his small team formed of male officers.

Andrew described his sudden anger and rage towards her; this anger culminated in an occasion where he came close to physically hitting and harming her. This incident prompted him to take a prolonged sick leave from work for the first time in a career of over thirty years.

In our therapy sessions, he stated that this woman colleague of his was not proving able to deal with her workload and was spending her workdays in endless lunch breaks. When I asked him what troubled him about her, he told me that he did not want to have to do her work, in addition to his.

'I do not wish to be *dumped* on,' he said.

At the beginning of our therapy sessions, Andrew had described himself as 'happily married'. He then told me that he had been married before, in his twenties, when he was at the beginning of his army career, and that his then wife had abruptly left him for another man from the army.

In this session when he was talking about his new woman colleague, 'I did not wish to be *dumped on,*' I was keeping silent, allowing him to continue, and he continued after a pause in his thought and referred to the divorce from his first wife with a particular word:

'I think I was *dumped* back there in my youth by my first wife, wasn't' I?'

The remark about his ex-wife came out of nowhere, and the words he used were unexpected; I could not help myself in saying: 'Yes, I am afraid you were.'

Andrew found some link between his new female colleague and his ex-wife whom he hated. And the words, the signifiers, were (also) part of this link.

II. MINDFULNESS IS FOR PSYCHOLOGISTS

Promise to my patients.

I cannot love you today
My soul is falling;
And faltering.
Today you have to love yourself
But I shall love you again tomorrow, even after five.

From *Journal of a Melancholic*, unpublished

I like to sometimes steal upon my patients; when I go to collect them from the waiting room on quiet afternoons in some large or small NHS buildings, as they are on their phones or reading something, unaware of my presence. I lean against the wall, I wait for them, while sharing the silent moments with them.

Usually they discover my presence quite soon and they seem a bit surprised, a bit amused, but never annoyed.

In our talks, I try to really listen and really pay attention. If thoughts not related to therapy cross my mind, I become aware of them and allow them to drift. Unfortunately, it's not only thoughts; often there are heavy feelings, during and after listening to their life stories about trauma, loss, pain.

Therapy means paying attention and bearing witness. And how can we bear witness unless we are being there?

'To my mind, the question for psychoanalysis is precisely how to be a witness, how to keep faith with this excess and abundance of suffering, over and beyond representation,' writes the psychoanalyst Rob Weatherill in his book *The Sovereignty of Death*.

While we carry around all the knowledge and categories we have learnt about, we need to still try and see how patients see the world and to never let our own ideas and beliefs substitute for their own. But how can we be sure that we never judge, since we remain human beings?

One patient I worked with at an NHS Mental Health Service in North-East London, Paul C., a man in his forties who suffered from severe depression, told me that all his life he felt desire for his own mother; to him she was the most beautiful woman and he felt conscious physical, sexual attraction to her.

Paul only told me about this when I glimpsed a faded photo of a naked woman on a postcard he was carrying in his wallet and asked him what it was. He told me that the picture resembled his mother faithfully; he had carried that picture with him since his early youth.

I remember that I was quite taken aback by his statements about his attraction to his own mother, I remember my hands tightening on my pen and notebook, and trying to not give that away. It was the first time I had heard something like this while conducting therapy, and the only time, since it has not happened again since. I used to ask myself, in Paul's sessions: 'Is this an unconscious childhood phantasy that somehow has trespassed into consciousness?'

Paul stated that he felt that he also identified with his mother and that he felt that his effeminate side was very strong. He told me that sometimes, in his adult life, in his privacy, he would wear women's corsets and lingerie.

He described himself as heterosexual, and said that he was married, with three children. His wife had been a friend in his childhood and had grown up on the same street as he had. His childhood was a very rough one, where a cruel and abusive father subjected him and his tender and loving mother to his ill-treatment.

From his childhood, there were mostly memories about his father beating him. But one particular memory stood clear: witnessing his parents making love in the sitting room; Paul was about five years old at that time and was hidden in the dark, sitting at the top of the staircase. What he saw appeared to him as a rare moment of tenderness, as his father did not appear as violent as usual.

In our work together we turned to psychoanalytic techniques to look for answers; did Paul fail to identify with his own cruel father whom he loathed, did he seek his father's love and approval by identifying with his mother?

Paul stated he was much helped and relieved to learn about the concept of *Oedipus complex*.

After a limited number of therapy discussions (about twenty allowed to us by the NHS protocol) I confessed doubt at my ability to help him.

Paul said: 'You do not know how much you helped, it was the first time I could talk about this. You listened and you did not judge. I can now let go of the postcard.'

III. THE STRANGENESS OF LOVE

The end of Madness, the beginning of Truth. I don't think of you anymore. Forgotten. I have forgotten you so quickly. You must have been forgotten all along.

From *Journal of a Melancholic*, unpublished

Mark A., fifty-six-year-old, came to therapy because he believed, he said, that he wasted his life.

According to what he told me, all his life had been somehow entangled with that of a friend from his youth. His friend was married and had a daughter and a son.

Mark had been very close to his friend's family, helping with the care of the children, spending time with them and lending a substantial amount of money when his friend decided to move with his wife and children to the United States.

Because of this loan, which remained un-returned, Mark got into serious debt, had to become increasingly careful with his finances and had been working long shifts as an engineer at a power station for extra income. He had continued to be very close to his friend's family and visited them abroad two or three times a year, despite not being able to afford to do so within reason.

Mark told me that he had been very attracted to, and possibly 'in love' with his friend's wife, and that he had tried to support her through this marriage that was mostly unhappy. He became a mentor for the couple's two children, always helping them with never-ending practical issues and with money.

Mark never married and had very few and short-lived relationships which he described as 'friendships'.

However, after over twenty years of this particular friendship and attachment, when his friend and his wife returned to England and separated, Mark did not try to pursue her.

He had been dedicated to her all those years whilst she 'belonged to someone else'.

And it was then, in his late fifties, that he started to believe that he had wasted his life.

Sigmund Freud, in his *Contributions to the Psychology of Love*, tells us about some peculiar ways that men go about loving their preferred 'objects'.

First, he mentions those men who cannot want or love a woman unless that woman is not free, unless she is already committed or attached to someone else.

This would approximate what psychoanalysts would consider a 'hysterical' way of loving.

The man who is in the place of woman's other lover, or the husband, is the person with whom the prospective lover would have to wrestle in order to win their woman;

Freud, obviously, relates the other man to the image of the father.

Secondly, Freud tells us about those men who are drawn to fallen women, those described as 'dirne' (in German 'dirne' means a fallen woman, wanton or a courtesan/prostitute).

Freud also talks about a need in some men to debase the object of love in order to achieve full 'satisfaction'; he remarks about a fate of impossibility in love: 'Where one desires one cannot love and where one loves one cannot desire'.

We always find the idea of the impossibility of reconciling desire and love.

It is Sigmund Freud again who tells us, that after the loss of our primordial attachments, our need and desire become insatiable, eternally seeking out their lost object.

Subsequent and repeated 'objects of love' in our life are only substitutes that will never quench our lack; that is why one keeps needing, keeps desiring, keeps failing at holding onto objects of desire. That is why children seem to ask lots of questions. 'One question is the one they really want to ask but it never crosses their lips'. And that one question is: *Do you love me?* (Do you love only me? / Is it I who has your love?).

In his book on the *Psychology of Love*, Freud tells us that there are men who choose a virtuous woman as their object of (desire?) love, but he also states that this leads to inconstancy, that often these men achieve a series of such women, especially if they move or change their environment.

As for a woman, it appears (from my point of view as a psychologist) that her love is peculiar altogether.

She seems to love in man something which does not depend on the man completely, something beyond him, something that transcends the man. This renders the man totally irreplaceable, but easily substitutable.

Women could live without men. Women could demand and accept only what they wish and need, and leave the rest to fall by the wayside. They could demand tenderness, time, words, support and knowledge, which may prove more important than anything else. This could give women such strength and possibility, but this knowing is utilized in rare circumstances by women, and far too infrequently.

IV. ENCOUNTERS

Proximity of desire, or of something that makes me suffer with desire. It felt like falling, immaterial, all my being just dreams and memory.

If it was not for the pain of wanting you I would probably be glad of it. The violence of wanting you makes me ill, feverish. Drunk, surreal, mad.

From *Journal of a Melancholic*, unpublished

Apphia R., one of my patients, told me about something that happened at a time when she thought herself most in love, and engaged to be married. On an evening out with her best friend at a restaurant in Canary Wharf, she felt an overpowering curiosity and attraction for a stranger at a nearby table. She told me that something like this had not happened before, that she considered herself a faithful and loyal person, and, more than this, she thought she was very much in love with her fiancé.

She described the encounter as agony, not only because of a violent attraction, but also because of feelings of guilt, dismay, sadness.

The stranger in the restaurant remained a stranger and her engagement ended shortly afterwards.

When we discussed about her relationship and engagement, we came across aspects that were far from her ideal, things that in a way had worried her about the relationship from the beginning and which she was perhaps denying, or trying to not think about. Apphia was acknowledging that her fiancé was very self-involved, addicted to computer games outside work and that their relationship was mainly physical, with very rare discussions between them or exploring each other's personality.

She told me that the stranger she had felt so attracted to appeared to be a business man, in a meeting with colleagues, and that she was struck by the way he seemed to listen and interact with his colleagues, and that there was a certain 'seriousness' about him. Apphia remarked during our therapy discussions that, 'Had I not seen that stranger that night, I would have probably invented him'.

It seemed very important that the stranger seemed to Apphia to have qualities that her fiancé did not possess. This short encounter nevertheless changed her life as it led to her breaking off her engagement. I could not help thinking about the timing of this encounter, a couple of weeks before the engagement party. Although it was a missed encounter, it was nevertheless, a most powerful one.

Within life, we are sometimes given encounters, situations, words and people that we did not expect to come across.

These encounters will be lost amongst memories if we do not choose and decide to do something and act upon them.

This may be quite a difficult task as it is precisely in situations like this when our anxiety, fear or avoidance may take over. We might think the worst things about ourselves in situations like this. We perhaps see ourselves from the outside in a critical manner. But if we are aware of this, we may try to suppress this imaginary, watchful, critical eye that is set on us at all times, but especially in social situations.

We can imagine that we are aliens, or undercover agents, or that we are invisible, so what we do and say does not have lots of importance as long as we remain respectful – warning: do not try to harm others. Just try and be there, and, if possible, talk.

Put yourself in a new role – if you were a mouse or a rabbit, would you be embarrassed about talking to or engaging others?

The French philosopher Alain Badiou talks about the choice we have in life and love, the choice to declare one's love, to work at love. He states that, 'a declaration of love transforms chance into destiny'.

His ideas about the need to work at love remind us of our fundamental ability and duty to choose and decide how we go about our life and actions.

A reminder, that we can try and take a different path in each moment of life, that we can decide to take a new path in each moment of life. Speaking to others may be difficult, but we can start by lingering, by not leaving, by being present to the source of our desire.

.

V. ON LOSS AND LOVE

All this beauty begging at my feet. I cannot fall for it, because my soul has already fallen and it's already fractured.

There are times of unbelievable beauty, when beauty is redundant, unwanted and wasted.

I am so grateful, for the memories inflicted on my soul.

From *Journal of a Melancholic*, unpublished

One of my patients, Sophie, a woman in her late twenties, told me about attending a seminar the previous weekend. 'It was so cold on Saturday afternoon, and although I was hoping to go for a walk in Bloomsbury, I decided to attend the Philosophy seminar at Berkeley University instead. It was a seminar about Discourse Ontology.

'I was talking to a colleague from the seminar and I sat in the first row. When the three lecturers arrived and took their seats, I was watching them when something very strange happened. I was looking at one of the lecturers and felt this very curious emotion. How can I describe it?… You may say that I was attracted to him, but it felt very overpowering. There was a feeling of intense sadness, something heavy as though something was pulling me down and grounding me heavily to the floor. There was also a strange sense of excitement, a sort of recognition of something I could not understand. It felt very physical as though it was happening in all my body. I was not sure I felt something similar before, although I had felt attraction before, and I had also felt in love before.'

I asked Sophie about this lecturer. She told me that the lecturer appeared to be from Greece, by the name and accent, and that he had a crooked nose.

'I think I have always been attracted to men with a crooked nose. I cannot explain the curiosity I have for them.'

'Why a crooked nose', I asked Sophie, 'whom does someone with a crooked nose remind you of?'

'It does not remind me of someone in particular... I cannot remember any relatives, or family friends with a crooked nose. My father, who was so handsome, had a straight nose, and not a crooked one. Strangely, now that I come to think of it, my mother has a somewhat crooked nose...'

After a long pause, Sophie continued: 'When I was little, I used to devour books on Greek mythology. I was completely in awe, all I wanted was to live in Greece. I remember that I came across a poem that said that ancient Greeks had a crooked nose...'

For Sophie, her *objet petit a* (an *elusive mark* as I call it), the feature that most attracted her to someone, seemed to have been entangled with a signifier, a word that was linked to other realms, to knowledge, adventure, discovery.

O*bjet petit a* is one of the most important notion in psychoanalysis; a complex notion that relates to excess remainder, to that which we take or enjoy beyond and outside the utility of our actions, to what inspires our search for something and for someone, to what guides desire.

Objet a is related to a primordial loss of an ideal relationship, it is related to what we continue to search for in life, it is related to phantasy and desire. It is a lost image that is kept in our hearts.

Objet petit a, this impossible *elusive mark*, constitutes a frame for what we will find attractive in others in our lives. In other words, when we are attracted to someone, this is not entirely by chance.

When we are attracted to someone, this is not entirely their credit. It is the lack in ourselves, it is a void in ourself that we sometimes try to fill with something or someone. But this something or someone needs to resonate with that *something* that has been inscribed in us. They need to resonate with an image, with a feeling, with words that have become part of us, with words that are part of our unconscious structure; they need to resonate with our *elusive mark.*

They need to resonate with our fundamental phantasies, where phantasy takes on the dimension of the core of our emotional life, a core that we are highly unaware of. This core acts like a script for us, a frame that we have for unravelling our life.

It may seem superficial, but this means that a small feature, a gesture, a way with words can attract us to someone. But it has to be that one feature, gesture, way with words that has been imprinted on our psyche. Even though most often we are unaware of this, that precise physical or behavioural feature of another will act as a catalyst for our desire.

The *elusive mark* may have something to do with our early years, our parents, or even the first people that we have loved, perhaps even the kindergarten boy or girl that we played with. But why did we like them so at that early age? Have they, too remembered us of someone, of something, or it was pure chance, proximity, purity and vulnerability of the soul?

A primordial past is present in us and always alive.

In the book *Lacan On Love*, the Lacanian psychoanalyst Bruce Fink states that a psychoanalyst has to genuinely care and love their analysand. The word 'love' is used in terms of sharing knowledge, trying to help, trying to understand, liking the analysand.

The advice given by Fink is to not work with patients whom we do not like and love. This is because the patient would recognise the lack of love, the lack of care, and that would not help them, on the contrary, it may further harm them

The therapist, on the other hand, often becomes *objet petit a* for the analysand, only to be 'discarded', rejected at the end of the treatment.

Does our *objet a*, our *elusive mark* help us attain nearness to others, or does it get in the way of it?

Because of this *elusive mark*, we may not perceive others with all they possess, and we may fragment them in our minds. Is the *elusive mark* a divine quality, or a devilish one?

The *elusive mark* is that which attracts us to objects and people; its force is that of attraction, as though a magnet attracts metal; the *elusive mark* tragically, still, does not have enough power to hold us, to arrest us, to keep us.

VI. ON SILENCE

First letter.

The silence of the deserts is not enough for my amalgamated mind. I wish to gather all the sounds and leave them at your feet. Do with them as you will. In the translucent silence, the stars overthrow the days and their coldness burns a sapphire light. And all would be fractured forever with the first utterance of the name of the time.

From *Journal of a Melancholic*, unpublished

Rebecca A., a patient in her late thirties, said in the first session that she had completely stopped talking to her family, to her sister and her mother. Her father had passed away few years previously and this had been a very difficult time for Rebecca.

She said that her entire life she had a difficult relationship with her mother. She described her mother as a cold, distant person. Rebecca said that her mother never said anything good about her, not even when she started University or achieved something important like completing the doctorate in her medical career. Rebecca said that when she was young, her mother had never given her any advice about life, and in general her mother did not seem to spend any time with her at all. Her mother was a very good cook, however Rebecca said that she never learnt anything about cooking as her mother would often be impatient about Rebecca's presence in the kitchen and tell her to leave.

Her parents divorced when she was seven, and her mother remarried shortly afterwards. She said that she had lost her father twice, once through the parents' divorce, and then when he died. She lived with her mother, sister and stepfather in Yorkshire until the age of twenty-four when she moved to London.

Rebecca said that after the move she tried her best to maintain a relationship with her mother, visiting, bringing her gifts; however, she seemed to receive from her mother only criticism. She said that her mother used to criticise her for small things, such as her clothes, her haircut, or more important ones, such us travelling a lot for work, or being single.

Rebecca said that in the past years her mother was telling her off about negative traits that her mother believed Rebecca took from her father. When I asked what sort of traits she thought her mother meant, she tried to give me examples, she told me that if she had a glass of wine, her mother would tell her that she was most likely to become an alcoholic, like her father. If she would become annoyed when her mother was accusing her of being jealous of other people's successes, people whom, Rebecca said, she never even thought or talked about, but whom her mother compared her with, her mother would say that she most definitely inherited a violent temper from her father.

Rebecca said that she thought that her mother was a simple woman who had suffered a lot in her life therefore she did not want to add to this suffering by being distant or disrespectful. Her mother had suffered from breast cancer when Rebecca was a teenager and she often told Rebecca about her second husband's affairs and unfaithfulness. However, things became even more difficult in old age as her mother was diagnosed with psychotic depression and possibly paranoid delusions. It is possible that Rebecca had somehow become a target for her mother's mental health difficulties.

Rebecca said that her sister was a wealthy businesswoman who would scorn Rebecca for being fairly poor, and call her a 'loser'; her sister tried to use her in the past as a baby-sitter for her children, but never thanking her or inviting her to any of the children's birthday parties or other family events. In the last summer holiday before therapy started, Rebecca decided, with a heavy heart, to break all communication with her sister and her mother.

She told me in our therapy discussions: 'I felt that I could not find anything to say to them any longer. They were hearing my words not with love, but with resentment, almost with hatred. Whatever I was saying and doing seemed to get distorted, until I felt there was no point in saying anything any longer.'

We often try to understand why we are not loved, when we are not loved. Rebecca decided to try and understand, by starting therapy. But at the same time, she decided that it was not the most crucial thing to know the reason why she was not loved, but to acknowledge the lack of love, to acknowledge that nothing she had ever done or tried made her any more loved by her mother and sister.

According to existential psychologist Rollo May, 'Psychoanalysis, and any good therapy, is a method of increasing one's awareness of destiny in order to increase one's experience of freedom.'

The most important benefit from therapy seems to be, indeed, increased awareness of our fate. There is also awareness that in all relationships and communication we have an important option: to not reply, to not say anything at all.

We do not owe people words, answers and explanations. In therapy we often become aware that, in life, we have the choice to not answer to others' words at all.

VII. UNREQUITED LOVE

In the old town, snow has veiled buildings and trees, ugliness and beauty alike.

Only my soul does not render itself to be veiled; it remains burning and raw in the cold night.

From *Journal of a Melancholic*, unpublished

Before coming to see me for therapy in our Hampstead clinic, Walter used to live in a village in the country. A few years previously, when he turned fifty, he had sold his flat in Richmond and moved to a village near Cambridge. He had inherited from his uncle a beautiful cottage with old floorboards and fireplaces. His family, made up of his father and his brother, lived abroad in Israel.

He said that he felt tired of London. He would see his few friends in London occasionally and he had given up his teaching job as he tried to focus on writing a book.

After two years in the village, he joined a small reading club formed of five or six members with an interest in Philosophy. The host of the reading club was a woman in her fifties, and married, a woman whom Walter described as possessing of a striking beauty.

Walter fell in love with her from the first day.

'Something like that has not happened to me since I was in my twenties,' Walter said when we started working together in therapy following his return to London.

'I used to think of her all the time, I was only going to this book club and reading boring books so I could see her. A smile, a word, would sustain me through weeks on end. She did not seem to respond to me.

I could not really focus on my writing.'

'Why did I have such propensity? Why did I love someone who did not respond to me?' Walter asked in therapy.

Whilst we can never answer such questions, it may be relevant that Walter grew up with his father and brother after his mother died from illness when he was a six-year-old. Walter said he had precious memories of a very gentle and loving mother, who was very beautiful.

He said that this was an ideal that he did not find later on in life.

It may be relevant also that he loved books and Philosophy, and that he fell for someone who loved books and Philosophy too.

Walter told me that there was some sort of event in his story: 'After almost two years of this torment of wanting her, and tired of the isolation of life in the village, I have decided to return to London, especially as my brother's son was planning to start attending University here. In my last month in the country I thought of attending the book club to say farewell to my reading friends. I wanted to see her and spend a few more hours in her nearness. I had given up completely on any idea and hope of being with her. But it so happened that on that last evening, a stormy November evening, no one else was there but her.

Did she know? Had she known all along? We had some wine, we talked about our lives and we kissed... we ended up spending most of the night embraced on the floor. It was the happiest night of my life.'

In Buddhist teachings, lust (as well as hatred) is considered 'an affliction'. This same idea is to be found in psychoanalytic theory, with Jacques Lacan's teaching that, 'for man, a woman is a symptom; for woman, man is an affliction.'

This is a reminder that, in relating to others, we bring our deepest vulnerabilities and struggles. Desire can be a force that will affect our life and torment us.

And when has life been free of lust and desire?

I would like us to distance ourselves from any attempt of judging love and affection, and to get closer to bringing more awareness into it.

I want us to be reminded that we can try to look at our feelings and be aware of how we feel, of what we make of what's happening, and of how we respond.

Let's not talk about happy relationships just yet. Let's talk about unhappy relationships where one person gives too much and does not receive much in return; the ones where one tries too hard; where one tries to change him or herself in order to make the other happy or more content; the ones where desire is fading. The list is so long.

Some may argue that objectivity has nothing to do with love and lust; but sometimes we limit or even stop ourselves from wanting someone when we learn of the impossibility of a relationship with them.

Of course, *la douleur exquise* (a French concept similar to unrequited love) still occurs, but I am trying to highlight that, even with intense feelings, some streak of reason can still be exerted.

Unrequited love can have intense reverberations; it will make us persist in it. It is a love most useful to poets and writers, but if we are not poets, what are we going to do with it? Nothing can force someone to love us in return; nothing can change the absence of their love for us.

Not persuasion, not words, not jealousy, not suffering. We cannot force affection, and it is useless to try.

We may think that someone is unattainable, and this would give them a terribly high status in our eyes.

Reasoning and awareness can allow us to recognise that no one is truly unattainable or inappropriable. That the people that we may desire and cannot 'have', are being 'had' by other people, often in quite easy and prosaic ways.

VIII. ON WAYS
OF LOVING

Maybe days were made for sleeping
And hatred for loving
But you got me confused
I love and hate and love every memory
Of you.

From *Journal of a Melancholic*, unpublished

In every relationship we bring old patterns, old love, old hatred. Love for our first caregivers, love for important people in our life.

If someone jokes that 'if someone likes me, it's because I have something familiar to them,' they are probably quite close to a truth.

Returning to Freud, he explains in his *Contributions to the Psychology of Love*, that for men, it all seems to stem from childhood, and I believe for women as well. (If we keep to the ontic view, that is, as psychoanalysis does not seem to concern itself with the ontological.)

Imagine the little boy who develops his first attachment towards his mother. Freud states that repression of this originates from the authoritative figure of the father (instilling the so-called *fear of castration*, and later leading to identification with the father).

But let us try and figure out what is happening with the boy's love and desire.

In his early years he learns that his mother is not his alone, but that his mother prefers and desires something else, someone else, beyond him, someone who is classically the father but could perceivably be the mother's work or life interest.

Quite simply, this love the child has for the mother can easily turn to hatred. A hatred likely repressed in the unconscious.

Jacques Lacan talks about the entanglement between love and hate and develops the concept of *hainamoration* from merging the two concepts. This is a powerful reminder that hate is always a part of love; indeed, sometimes, hatred is stronger than love.

Sigmund Freud taught that, according to our *narcissistic style,* we love in others:

Something we have
or
Something we used to have and we have lost
or
Something we wish we had.

Or, according to *our attachment style*, we love:

The woman who looked after us
or
The father who protected us.

It may help to keep in mind that relationships are so incredibly complicated and that under the surface they are deep like icebergs. If someone likes us because we bring familiarity, one may equally not like us because that same familiarity is lacking. Or, there is familiarity of a negative sort (we remind them of hurtful things and people).

Such awareness brings humbleness.

If someone wants us, it is not entirely of our making. Similarly, if someone does *not* want us, it is not entirely on us. If someone does not want us any longer, we may or may not have a fault in that.

However, love should always carry some rationality, and some aspect of personal decision. It is often the case that we stop desiring someone who is 'taken' or unavailable, exactly because we impose some sort of control over our desire. In the same vein, we can also decide to pause, stop or distance ourselves when things 'do not feel quite right.'

Ambivalence seems to be a constant in affection. Love and hatred are very closely entangled and part of an inner dialogue.

For some people hatred is given primacy over love, such persons are looking in others for reasons not to love, *but to hate, or to be hated*.

Obviously, sometimes control is not possible and we are carried by passion. Carried into complicated affairs or unrequited love.

Love is addictive. We always want more.

We often neglect to be grateful even for the shortest of durations, even in the fleeting moments we have with someone we desire.

Time is precious; a day, a week, or a month shared with someone is something to behold and to treasure, even though our hope was for the 'eternal.'

I don't mean to say that I am encouraging short or casual 'relationships' here, but am referring to moments when we get to really talk to someone, smile at them, contemplate them, and share a dream or an interest with them.

I am always astounded at youthful hopes of 'being with someone for the rest of our life.' What youthful arrogance!

Awareness and therapy can bring more clarity and objectivity to our relationships.

We often focus on one's qualities but neglect to consider any flaws. Then again, depending on our personality, we often see flaws everywhere.

In therapy, it often helps to increase awareness that relationships gather many ambiguities.

Jacques Lacan famously said that, 'love means giving what we don't have.' It is a statement that reminds us that we love from the position of what is missing in us, not from what we possess. A reminder about the difficulty, if not the impossibility, of Love.

When we love, we wish to give happiness, even when we do not have it ourselves. We wish to make someone happy even when we are unhappy ourselves.

We may look in the loved ones for something that they are lacking but which we bestow upon them; in order to be able to love, the lover has to bestow on the beloved something that he himself has borrowed, from gods, from fate.

And gods are stingy, they lend to only the few fortunate ones; love is a miracle that happens once in a blue moon.

So much has been said and written about love, and yet, love eludes explanation and classifications. The more we write about and clarify Love, the clearer it becomes that we do not know about it and we do not understand it, in its mysterious, divine or devilish nature.

Love is..

IX. LANGUAGE AND THE UNCONSCIOUS

The silence in the journal was my slipping further into madness. The limit with the rain and trees is more and more blurred.

But writing here I am reminded that I am not a tree.

From *Journal of a Melancholic*, unpublished

David R., fifty-eight-year-old, was not someone whom a psychoanalyst would call a *neurotic structure* (in Psychoanalysis, main structures are considered to be: neurotic, melancholic, psychotic and pervert).

He was more on the paranoid side, more of a 'psychotic' *psychological structure*. His constant worry was that his identity would be stolen by the Government, so he avoided using computers or credit cards altogether.

His preferred pastime was walking. He was very fond of London, especially the East End where he lived.

He was terrified about the idea of moving to the countryside, as his fiancée kept pressuring him to do. She had already rented a holiday home in the Norfolk countryside, where David's mother also lived.

David would often tell me about the weekends in the country.

'There is nowhere to walk, the road suddenly ends. The people have nothing better to do than to stop you in the street and talk to you. They never seem to be busy with anything'.

David seemed irritated by others' idle way of living. Apart from long walks, he was spending his time trying to edit some cherished journals and writings left to him by his father, which was a difficult task that was compounded further by his reluctance to use a computer.

He would describe the vibe of London's West End, which he occasionally visited, the feeling that he was part of something alive and vibrant.

As his partner Jane was approaching retirement from her teaching work, David was more and more concerned that he would have to choose between living with her in the country or separating.

Jane owned her own house in Hornchurch, and David owned a flat. David was never comfortable with being at his flat on his own. He would have done anything to stay at Jane's house, even sleeping on the floor when Jane's daughter and friends were at the house.

When at his flat, he would try to make no noise at all, as his downstairs neighbour used to make a great deal if any noise was heard. David was terrified by this neighbour. He expressed lots of thoughts that were more on the side of persecutory ideas. His biggest regret and confessed guilt was that of persuading his parents to sell their London house and move to the countryside. David was hoping that one day he might buy his former family house back. In his walks, he often passed by this house and stood there to contemplate it.

David often spoke of how Jane had refused his marriage proposals, some seventeen years before, shortly after they had met. He would tell me about their cold sexual embraces and how he felt that he was 'repulsive' to her.

In one session I asked him: 'What if you have to separate when Jane moves to the Norfolk village?'

David said: 'I cannot even think of this. Even if she does not want me, I am still her fiancé, a fiancé... If I was not this, I would be nothing at all.'

Language and speech play a dictatorial role in our life.

Psychoanalysis talks a lot about the role of the Unconscious in our life.

Our unconscious is more or less formed of Language itself.

One tries to fill in the role given to them by language. They try to be a husband, a fiancé, a mother or an employee, by following the prescription of that role, as understood or learnt.

Few people have their 'own' ideas about a role in their life. Most of our ideas are given by our learning, language and society. We do not fulfil the role of an employee in our own idiosyncratic, special way but only to a certain extent; certain things are demanded of us and imposed on us; we also bring some particularities from our own personalities and, most often, we try to adjust and adapt to demands.

We take some liberties as well, and some risks.

We are lost at the sea of language.

Immersed in language, there is no escape for us.

X. FOR WHOM
WE SPEAK

Falling on the side of the world. If world is a pretence, a façade, I always seem to fall outside this frame, to a world of shadow. There is no meaning there, but to me, falling is the meaning of the world.

From *Journal of a Melancholic*, unpublished

In psychoanalytic tradition, the act of speaking is considered a demand, a request for love. It is a request for attention, for being listened to.

I would like to think that speaking means also a manifestation of love, an act of giving something of ourselves.

We always seem to say *more or less* than what we mean to say. Somewhere, sometimes, in our words, something deeply true about us is being said. When we speak, we speak both with our consciousness, and with our unconscious side. When we speak, we also listen to ourselves, to what we say; we listen with both our conscious and our unconscious self.

That is why it is important for our words to be just and kind, since words have such heaviness not only on others but also upon ourselves.

Therapy encourages us to pay attention to the words we use, to the times we choose to speak at, to the times of silence.

When we speak to others, it may not even be them that we are addressing at all. We may in fact speak to or for someone else, for someone important in our past or in our current life.

Sometimes we tell someone something that is, at conscious or unconscious level, meant for someone else altogether.

We speak sometimes because we unconsciously wish or need to say something that has already happen.

And, we may never know that some casual or simple words of ours can bear much heaviness on another's life.

My patient, Hamid A., an African diplomat in his forties, had been arrested in a case of misrecognition. His details and physical features resembled those of someone wanted by the Police for a rape and murder case.

In our therapy sessions, I constantly felt that he was addressing not me, but someone beyond me, perhaps all of the people, the society and the world.

Arrested somewhere in Kent on charges of murder, Hamid had been transported in a Police van to Charing Cross Police Station on a hot July day.

He spoke about the shock of being accused of the murder of a young girl; it seemed surreal, an absurd thing that he was not able to understand.

His protests were not listened to, and further interviews and investigations followed.

Hamid described his distress at not being able to disentangle his identity from that of the wanted murderer.

Held in arrest for eight days and faced with continuous interrogation, he suffered complete 'alienation and madness', as he stated in therapy afterwards.

After his eventual release, when the murderer had been apprehended, Hamid's world changed completely.

Not trusting his wife any longer, who had not proved supportive of him and continuously asked, 'to know the truth about what happened,' he moved away from the family home, leaving also his seven-year-old son.

He was now living in a small flat in Maida Vale, and would become completely isolated. He repeatedly requested illness leave from work and was eventually suspended from his diplomatic duties.

Hamid became quite suspicious of strangers, especially the 'white ones', always looking over his shoulder in the street. He felt that what had happened was also because he was of black African descent. He intended to found an organisation to support people who go through similar experiences of misrecognition.

He described the arrest as the most traumatic event of his life.

In our talks, more and more memories emerged about his life as a child in Ghana, an African country torn by political violence, a time when life did not seem to have any value and when people's identities could crumble from one moment to next.

The mistaken arrest had unexpectedly exposed the frailty of his current life, and instability of his sense of identity.

As this crumbling event came from the outside, from the Other, the position of the Other was now held in complete doubt.

Hamid often spoke about those hours of being transported to the Police Headquarters, and the time spent in arrest, when he was uncertain whether he could prove his innocence, thinking that he might be accused of someone's death and lose his freedom and family.

After his release, there was shame, fear, anger, bewilderment. He took legal action against the Metropolitan Police, which he felt acted with complete disregard for his human rights.

Hamid spoke with difficulty about the eight days of 'angst and madness' whilst under arrest, but also aloneness, as his wife did not visit him.

Still, he wanted to disentangle a memory from the other memories, a memory about hope. A Police Officer had asked him, on the four-hour journey in the Police van on that hot summer day, whether he was thirsty, and offered him his own bottle of water.

XI. MELANCHOLIA

I miss you
But I cannot cry
Because I don't know if it would be for you
Or for everything I have ever lost.

From *Journal of a Melancholic*, unpublished

Abby, a patient in her mid-thirties, told me from our first discussion that everything that made her happy was entangled with a feeling of sadness and loss.

She told me about the most important relationship of her life, and being in love with a colleague of hers, four year younger than her.

She talked about the first days of their relationship; after some years of liking each other from a distance, every time she would receive a text message from her boyfriend, she said that her 'heart would smile'. She said that sometimes she would delay reading the message for a while, to postpone and prolong the joy. But, each and every time she received a beautiful message she would feel 'heart-breaking sadness'. She seemed to always think of the foreseen end of their relationship.

She had many unclear thoughts about a possible end of the relationship, that she tried to express in our therapy talks: 'There will come a time when I shall receive no more messages from him in the morning. These sweet messages will be no more.'

Abby said that these were messages that lovers sent to each other, just to say good morning or to tell about the longing of each other. Silly messages that did not mean much to anyone else, and in which, occasionally, lovers become poets. A simple text, repeating words, was turning into a poem. In a session, she scrolled in her phone in showed me some texts: 'Thinking of you, thinking of you...'

But it appears that there was never pure joy about them, the feelings of loss and sadness were present in every message of love.

She said that after the first night they had spent together, she felt happy, but tearful. She tried to explain what she felt: 'I was certain that I could never be happy in this way again, that our being together can never be as tender as it was, that it will be impossible for us to have whatever we had, again; I was certain that I had lost something really precious, though I had come very close within its reach..'

The feeling of loss was interwoven with everything in Abby's life, and with every moment of joy.

Abby was a melancholic.

In general, melancholics appear to see beyond phantasy and illusion; perhaps they see objects and people more clearly; they can perceive the lack in others, the fact that the others are, as all humans, imperfect and flawed. This realisation comes with disappointment and suffering.

Melancholics, most likely, have already been through the actual painful loss of someone most loved earlier in their life.

They may have experienced the death or loss of parents or siblings, or the loss of their home.

A loved person will bring into actuality the memory of loss, especially at unconscious level. In this way, melancholia is primordial longing, the sorrow of a primordial loss.

In philosophy, Plato talks about 'ideal forms' or ideal essence; all things, no matter how low, such as dust and mud, or high, such as animals and beings, have been replicated after an ideal mould.

Perhaps the nostalgia of the ideal mould never fades. This nostalgia can fatally overlap with melancholia. Someone we meet may 'remind' us in a metaphysical way of an ideal, of a pure idea. The closeness to, and loss of such ideal could result in melancholia, or what today we would call depression.

Melancholics seem to be able to possess an object of desire through its very loss. Remaining with the loss, inside that loss, will be the only possibility of keeping or continuing to keep the loved object.

Does this not render the melancholics as the most lucid of lovers? They are most aware that we cannot actually grasp, that we cannot possess what we desire, that all falls under the fate of loss.

Is it also possible that, in Melancholia, the loved person/object of love is perceived as lost before it is actually lost?

Treating an object of love as already lost can build an attempted defence against renewed suffering. (Also, this may represent a defence against being loved.)

Melancholics are able to find ecstasy in memories, and the pain of loss is juxtaposed with their refuge in memory. There is a refusal to let go of memories. The present does not offer the same passion; the present is no rival to a primordial past.

Melancholics desire with violence, and their desire turns upon themselves into a wound.

Melancholics have possibly lost more than any others. Their fate is a fate of loss.

In Melancholia, we forget God, but at the same time, we place ourselves completely into his mercy.

Melancholics are those who, while alive, are continually surrendering to death; in this surrender to death, life can truly be manifested.

XII. PASSION

Anamorphosis
2017

I am looking askew at memories
and cannot tell if they were happy
or unhappy.

From *Journal of a Melancholic*, unpublished

In 2019 I started working for a NHS Pain Management Service, with patients who were all suffering from chronic pain in their body.

As part of the assessment, I had to ask them when their difficulties with pain had emerged; for many of them, the problems with pain started when something else was lost, when some very important relationship ended, when work became unbearable or when there was no hope of solving a life situation.

In one case, a male patient in his early fifties started his first session by saying: 'I am not good with words. I cannot put feelings into words, and cannot really express how I feel.'

When I asked him about the start of his pain he answered: 'After my mother died. I was so close to her. I cannot say how it is to live without her'.

A woman in her forties, during our first session on a dark rainy afternoon, told me about a man whom she had dated and who assaulted her and broke her arm; this happened after she reproached him for dating other women at the same time as dating her, and hiding this from her. She said that she was blaming herself for not seeing the truth about his character, and for not telling her son the truth about what happened. 'I told my son that I broke my arm in a fall, and it is hurting me so much that I lied to him. I have never lied to him before,' she said in session. Even after the broken arm healed, the pain stayed on, together with the guilt.

Another patient, a lady in her late sixties, told me that she never loved her husband. She

A BOOK OF DESIRE

instead had some sort of life-long infatuation for her next-door neighbour. When her neighbour lost his wife and became a widower, he started to spend lots of time in their home, coming over for lunch and chats.

But she was not free to be with him; it was at this time that severe pain problems took over her body.

The psychoanalytic concept of *Jouissance* (a term introduced by Jacques Lacan) means the entanglement of pleasure and pain: *Jouissance* is suffering but also taking some sort of (hidden) pleasure, and finding some meaning, in that suffering. Jouissance is similar to passion. Passion means suffering.

Some people show a tendency towards passion, towards pain and suffering. It often seems that we are seeking pleasure and enjoyment, yet there is a point where we trespass into suffering. Trespassing brings passion, the possibility of higher pleasure, and with that higher pleasure, suffering.

Some of us strive for the excess in all that we do.

It seems that there is seldom excess without suffering and suffering, without excess.

It is possible that some of us are looking unconsciously for a bigger fall, from a higher height.

But what about those who do not look to fall, those who are staying in low, abusive, humiliating situations? It is possible that they find some meaning in these. They somehow find some reward in the suffering, in the martyrdom.

Mystical ecstasy, renunciation, abstinence, self-flagellation, over-use, they all have something in common with Jouissance, with Passion, with finding meaning in suffering, with finding suffering in meaning.

XIII. ON WEALTH

Storms of petals are not random. The trees are wasted and sorrowful.

From *Journal of a Melancholic*, unpublished

Wealth is not always enough in life.

A patient of mine, Joseph S., forty-nine, heir to a family that owned land and buildings in London's Mayfair district, was proof of this.

He was someone who could never have moments of silence in our therapy meetings.

I was always taken in with his stories, they were beautifully told. Something was always happening to him, and the sessions with him were always a tale. Joseph was the chair of various committees and organizations, also the owner of old buildings and beautiful racehorses. He would tell me about the restoration of historical buildings, his trips, collections of paintings of famous painters that came with their own history and that had to be sent to museums and public and private exhibitions around the world. This week would be about the mishaps in finding a retired pianist as a piano teacher for his daughters, another week about a hunting trip to Scotland.

The worst times for him were those when he was stuck all by himself.

One day before coming to therapy, Joseph's car broke down on a quiet and hidden lane in the countryside. Being on his own for a few hours, stuck in a place of silence and waiting for rescue, he suffered a heart attack.

Joseph told me that he had always been fond of telling stories, ever since he was sent to boarding school at the age of eleven.

I wanted to know about his time going to boarding school, and how the school had been, but he would not give me the chance to interrupt a story from the week.

After a few sessions I started to worry that I would never get the chance to say anything at all to Joseph or to intervene in sessions.

My supervisor reassured me and asked me to try and talk about this with him, but I could only listen as I never really had the chance to talk with him.

In his referral letter I read that he had a medical diagnosis of 'manic-depressive disorder'.

After a while, I was resigned that our discussions will continue in the same way: Joseph would tell me interesting or amusing stories, and I would listen to him.

I also resolved to ask for his file from his psychiatrist at the Priory Hospital in London, as a substitution for our missing dialogue.

When the file arrived a few days later, I had learnt that, at the age of eleven, Joseph went through a heart-breaking trauma. He witnessed the suicide of his father who shot himself with a hunting rifle.

The file allowed me to learn that Joseph was sent by his mother to a boarding school, then attended military school and went on to achieve further studies in Oxford.

He married and had three children and became a very successful businessman who maintained and increased a family fortune.

I started to wonder then if what helped and sustained Joseph, and was of most use in life to him, was his immense wealth, or the life he maintained through stories.

I confess that I easily get discouraged when I read books written by Buddhist teachers.

Most of them seem to start with the universal idea that people look to avoid suffering and to find happiness.

For someone like me who is in clinical practice, this is an idea that I find too simplistic.

In my clinical work I have come to see that many people repeat behavioural patterns that seem to produce pain and suffering.

Others engage in self-retribution patterns that are based on unconscious feelings of guilt.

Others will accept and remain for many years in unhappy or even abusive relationships and situations.

Others come under the term of masochism, either related to their sexual inclination, or moral masochism.

Wealth (or possessing financial means, or spending less) seems to be important in freeing us from the demand and desire of the other. Wealth is important in making us less susceptible to be owned, or used. But, unless we inherit, there will also be a high price to pay for building wealth.

In his philosophy book *The Republic*, Plato retells us the Myth of Er. It is an allegory for the fate of souls after death. Souls get to choose their next embodiment; after death we get to choose from animals' bodies and ways of life, or from famous people's ways of life, or from ordinary people's forms of life.

I believe that, in a similar way we can make this choice in our life. We can choose the way of life that we want most, and that is also possible to us. We can choose traits that are in keeping with a beautiful soul.

We can choose integrity, passion, and even retaliation and revenge, because in our chosen way of life, we are going for what we want most, and whilst we would never hurt others, we would never, ever allow others to hurt us.

XIV. ON TAKING OUR TIME

We ran out of time, for time, in time

From *Journal of a Melancholic*, unpublished

'Of all ridiculous things in the world, what strikes me as most ridiculous of all is being busy in the world, to be a man quick to his meals and quick to his work. For what do they achieve... Are they not like the housewife who, in confusion at the fire at her house, saved the fire-tongs? What else do they salvage from the great fire of life?'

Søren Kierkegaard, *Either/Or*

Nowadays, we are always rushing. We always have something to do, we always need to get somewhere.

The problem with rushing is that we overlook choice. In each moment we have choices, in each moment we have a repertoire of responses and actions available to us.

In therapy, we try and take our time. One of the 'strategies' we borrow from cognitive therapy is called 'imaginal exposure'.

For people who talk about their worries, we choose to actually construct a script in which to imagine the story of the worst worries coming true.

Stewart D., a patient in his mid-thirties, was always worrying that some accident would befall his new home; he agreed to imagine and write a script in which a load-bearing wall in his house would collapse.

Although it terrified him to engage with the story, he went on with it, he imagined how he would feel, and how he would react in such a situation; he imagined how he might deal with the situation.

He thought of how he might call the insurance companies, how he would ask his friends to come and help.

He spent time reading and rereading this feared scenario and stated that in time, imagining that this fear came true, he actually felt more assured by his own strength, and got some sense of power knowing that he could possibly deal with a problem, and being reminded that he could rely on others for support.

He said that eventually his fear subsided and that he, 'got bored with his worries'.

This strategy is based on a choice, the choice of doing the opposite of what we (the fearful ones) had done so far. Instead of avoiding what we fear, we choose to look fear in the face, to remain with it and even ponder it.

A psychoanalytic approach would have uncovered Stewart's fear and anxiety about the illness of his father and the painful fear of losing him. We would have tried to express this fear with words.

If we take our time, we can always think of alternative choices; when we find ourselves under pressure, our mind might benefit from this training.

Psychoanalysis is not entirely aloof from other forms of therapy or from philosophy. They come together sometimes, and other times they go their separate ways. They give each other what they do not have.

XV. COURAGE

*Haematopoiesis. We get new blood every day.
Can you feel it in you?*

From *Journal of a Melancholic*, unpublished

My forty-year-old patient Leyla had a 'repulsion for being desired'.

In all her love history, she had either loved unrequitedly, or she had flown away each time someone expressed strong interest or desire for her.

Her early life story was one marked by the absence of love.

Her few memories of her father were of an extremely loving father; however she had lost him at the age of five, when her mother left the family taking the two daughters with her. Leyla had an older sister with whom she had a cold and distant relationship.

Later on in life, there was no more love.

Her mother used to be reasonably caring whilst in the first marriage. Leyla had memories of her mother feeding her, looking after her tenderly on few occasions when she was ill. But then, lots of memories about her mother's absence. She remembered being looked after by an elderly neighbour because her mother was at work. Also she remembered in her adult life that her family was wealthy through her father's work, and wondered why her mother had to work such long hours. Her father was an architect and Leyla felt that she inherited from him a passion for buildings, for 'bricks and mortar', and stone. Although a surgeon, Leyla spent many years with two dilapidated houses that she bought and tried to fix and restore with the help of a builder friend's team.

She remembered her mother meeting a lover in a family friend's house when Leyla was four or five, the same man that her mother eventually married after leaving the father.

After leaving the father, her mother became completely cold, distant, and emotionally unavailable. Apart from food and shelter, no attention seemed to have been given to Leyla, no-one spoke to her, no-one used to ask her how school was, no-one bought her any clothes, toys or books.

Leyla took refuge in school work. At the age of five she started to learn to read and tried to read novels that were probably difficult to understand for a girl of her age. She told me that at the age of seven she was reading novels such as *The Three Musketeers*, and *The Mysteries of Paris*, and other novels borrowed from the local public library. She remembered being grateful that she had to wear a school uniform, for, outside school, she had no other clothes but some too large and baggy ones borrowed from her elder sister.

In her youth, she fell passionately in love with a young man with whom she barely spoke a few times. This un-returned love apparently lasted for years and years. She said that she was happy just to think of him, and have glimpses of him. Conveniently, he appeared un-attached, so she continued to hope for a long time.

After moving to London for her studies and work, she continued to fall in love with men who were unavailable, who were distant, absent, or married.

It was obvious that these were not simple crushes, as she continued to think about these men for months and even years on end and to even be faithful to them.

She also told me about a few times when she was wanted or loved by others.

She said that she used to find incredible faults in these men, and they could become totally undesirable after they expressed strong interest in her.

In our sessions she asked herself: 'I do not know, were the men who wanted me undesirable, or their desire for me made them undesirable?..'

It seemed to me, that whilst she grew up in the absence of love, and desperately thirsty for love, Leyla repeated later on in life the old way; she seemed to repeat the absence of love, and go towards lack of love, again and again. She was always in love with absence.

Not knowing how being loved feels, many of us do not even recognise love, or recoil from it altogether, or live all life without it.

In the end of therapy, Leyla made a choice, to distance herself from those intoxicating situations where her interest was not returned. She became better at recognising her vulnerability when going towards impossibility and absence.

She decided to linger with someone who seemed really interested in her, although in the beginning her first response was to become frightened and run away.

To me, that was courage.

Philosophy makes a distinction between anxiety and fear, and so does psychoanalysis.

Whilst anxiety appears to not have an object, fear seems to have an object: fear of, fear in the face of it.

Philosophers speak of fear as of forgetting of oneself, of forgetting all possibilities in fear. The philosopher Martin Heidegger reminds us that Aristotle regards fear as 'depression and bewilderment'. We are reminded that, in a burning house, because of fear and panic, people will save the things that are mostly indifferent, not important, the things that are 'close at hand'.

Indeed awareness of self seems to be dissociated from fear.

But what are we afraid of, when we are afraid? There could be fear of injury, fear of shame, fear of loss, fear of death.

We are sometimes afraid of losing something that we do not have anyway, or afraid of losing something that does not belong to us, or of losing something that has already been lost.

Often we forget that in frightful situations we are not in a life and death situation. The worst that can happen will be that we will get hurt. But we are always already exposed to being hurt in life. So if this is at risk, our physical and emotional integrity, we can stand up for ourselves. In a risk situation, people who wish to harm us will perceive our resolution to stand our ground and might even retreat.

Women especially will sometimes find themselves in situations where they should put up a life and death fight. We need to keep the belief that we should rather die than let something more terrible than death happen to us.

And then, the courage of wisdom, and of solitude.

XVI. SOLITUDE

Solitude is to always long, always hope, always despair. Self-imposed solitude – the need to always agonise.

..

Have You made me so lonely so I can love only You?

From *Journal of a Melancholic*, unpublished

Lots of us are afraid of, or uncomfortable with being on our own.

Often we accept the company of people we are not very sure of.

Often we go along with friends we are not necessarily crazy about, just to not be on our own.

Some people even marry people, in order to not be on their own.

For women, being on our own is always more complicated.

This is an email from a thirty-seven-year-old female patient who came to see me after the loss of her father. She was one of the relatively few patients who did not seem afraid to be on her own.

'Last week I was in Athens.

'I was happy to wander the streets, or stay in my sunny room, write in my journal and in my blog. In the morning I would go down to breakfast in my small hotel in this beautiful old building.

'I would make plans for the day and mark places on the map. I would savour my coffee with milk, and look out of the window.

'Sometimes when I travel I observe the others at the other tables. Some couples, some groups. They do not always seem to share something, and sometimes I cannot see their joy, no matter how hard I look.

'What I cherish most about travelling alone is going with the flow and not being totally touristy. Of course you feel the need to talk to someone sometimes, to say how beautiful, or not, you find something. But for this, if you really want to, you have the use of journals, social media, postcards, letters, messages to good friends.

'In Athens, as it is my second visit, I am deciding to not necessarily climb the Acropolis. I have unexpected views of it, glimpses from the streets that I wander daily. I am deciding in my head, that the Acropolis remains as an elusive object of desire, unreachable and dreamlike.

'But a few days before leaving Athens I wandered too close to the foot of the Acropolis, near Roman Agora. Being so close to it, and although it was late afternoon, I have decided to go all the way to the top. I do not know if it was because of the sun almost setting over it, the fading light, or the almost unexpected chance to see it, but, being on the Acropolis on that late April day felt out-of-this-world. On the top of the Acropolis, I was delirious with solitude.'

XVII. HOPE

One believes that he can make decisions, follow own paths. But life has a way of fracturing, it forces us to go one way; there is nothing to decide. Accept, look in the distance, watch your step. Perhaps it is all meant to happen exactly this way.

From *Journal of a Melancholic*, unpublished

My patient Sylvia was a beautiful seventy-two-year-old lady.

In one of our discussions on a sunny winter morning, she said that the previous weekend she had had a date with someone from an Internet dating website.

'We had lunch, and then we came back to my flat for coffee. He asked me to sit next to him, and then he tried to kiss me. I refused.

DR LIA T. ASANDEI

If he is like this from the first meeting, how will he be at the second?'

Sylvia had been married, and divorced at fifty-two. She had two children, a son and a daughter.

After the divorce, she had a relationship with a Jewish man ten years younger than her.

'I had such a romantic ideal...' she told me. 'He never told me that he loved me. But I was hoping that he would change his mind, that he would marry me. I did not wish to end up alone.'

Sylvia had become a Christian towards the end of her marriage, and stated that her recent faith gave her strength to put up with an unloving husband. She had stayed in the marriage for twenty-eight years, and left only when he increasingly demanded her to leave.

Sylvia now lived on her own in a small, rented flat in St John's Wood, in North London.

She taught English as a volunteer, attended art classes, attended church and spent time with her children, her grandchildren and her friends.

However her ideal of finding love had not left her. But she said that she would place it in divine hands, and not dating websites.

'If God has a plan for me, I will meet someone. I will not try to force this myself,' she said.

Sylvia recognised that she lived by a romantic ideal.

It seems to me that all of us live by an ideal, all of us seem to need an ideal to be able to stay alive. We share ideals with others.

What would we do without ideals? We would be overwhelmed by the frightfulness of life, we would have to create new armours and veils, but, unlike illusions, these would probably be more ours, our own creation.

The Bible tells us that after the fall from Eden, women were accursed, not only through the pain of childbirth, but also to have 'desire for the husband'.

But husbands' desire did not seem to be directed in the same way. Desire was, even from Biblical times, fated to be, asymmetrical.

XVIII. ON LANGUAGE

Language. There is so much love lost between people.

From *Journal of a Melancholic*, unpublished

Have you ever lived, have you ever been through something that you could not really put into words, or were not able to say more about beyond 'something happened'?

Some experience that you could not quite categorise, explain, or compare to anything else? Experiences that are nevertheless charged emotionally, but where even emotions seem strange and new?

There is no way to make sense of such events. These seem to be at the edge of meaning, outside language.

What can we do about these occurrences, rather than accept them, and allow them to be part of us?

We have to accept that there are 'things' that we cannot see, that we cannot understand, that we cannot put into words, or that will be forever hidden.

Although they seem to be made only of emotions, yet we can ascribe a time or place to them, but we cannot explain them with words. Feelings and emotions can function as another sense, a sense even for things that we cannot see and we cannot really know. If philosophers talk about essence, the thing in itself, the unknowable, there is no way of accessing these by our perceptions but it is not impossible that we access them by feelings, by our 'soul'.

Unknown things or situations are stored for us, in us, and we remember them. They are inscribed, etched in us. We remember how it felt, and that it felt in a certain way. Our memory of feelings and emotions ensure that they do not leave us.

Why should we assume that all human emotions are those recognised by psychology manuals? Could there not be more emotions, could we not have emotions and feelings forming at the edge of known emotions, between them, over or under them, compounding or fracturing them?

Not everything we feel in life can be found and explained on a page of a psychology manual or dictionary.

We have no way of knowing if other people feel in a similar way to us, even when we talk about a 'common emotion' such as anxiety.

In my clinical work, I started to doubt the existence of an 'unconscious'.

But of course we have language, and laws.

Language and laws dictate what we do or should do, sometimes even unbeknown to us.

We are given words with a certain meaning and we try to live up to that meaning.

The meaning of words places a demand on us, a command.

We are told and taught 'education', 'love', 'duty', 'good', 'bad'.

The word becomes inscribed in us, the meaning of words permeates and controls us.

To try and think for ourselves is to challenge the sense, is to challenge the meaning that words have, and to lend that challenge to our lives.

We often say certain words because we find hidden pleasure in saying them.

We often speak to a person, but in fact we may say to them something that is intended for someone else, or we say something that is intended for someone from our past, or is meant for ourselves.

We also have silence.

When we are around others we can choose to keep silent, even though we are still immersed within language. We can go to therapy and talk for a good hour, but we can also keep silent, be silent with our thoughts, in the presence of the other, in the presence of the Other.

The advice or the interpretation of the therapist is really helpful sometimes, but other times I wonder why they are saying what they are saying, which books and therapy models they have been following, whom they are taking after.

Would they give the same advice or interpretation to another?

Lots of books of philosophy try to deal with the concept of 'existence' and 'time'. What is 'existence'? What is 'time'? Well, first of all they are words that humans invented, we don't know how, we don't know when.

Some philosophers believe that old, ancient concepts bear profound truth. Just because these concepts are old, they should necessarily be deemed pure, closer to primordial truths, philosophers seem to say. And why should it be so? Do we go back to times when people mingled with gods? Do they believe that Divinity has given us language, and words?

It would be beautiful indeed to think that language was given to us as a divine gift. Although we have no recollection of this.

Language makes us stumble so often. Language fails sometimes when we try to say the most important things we wish to say.

My work with patients taught me that whoever has not suffered from the limitation of language and categories, has either not thought badly enough, or loved badly enough.

XIX. DEATH DRIVE

It has never rained like this before,
but rain does not touch me;
weary of flying, I am resting here
inside a memory
that I am waiting to happen
before I can let go.

From *Journal of a Melancholic*, unpublished

Lydia was a patient in her mid-thirties.

Of an unconventional, unusual beauty, she was highly educated, and had studied Law and Political Sciences at Paris and London Universities.

In our first discussions she told me that she never had a stable relationship. For many years she felt infatuation for a friend who was gay and who was in a relationship with another man.

She wished to live with them, but always felt that she was an outsider. However, she spent a few years as their housemate in the Lincolnshire countryside, trying her best to share their interests, and to be part of the life they had. After few years of living together, when Lydia was working away in London, the couple decided that they wished to have the house only for themselves, and did not continue to allow her to live with them.

One year later in London, Lydia met another couple formed of two gay young men with whom she decided to rent and share a large house in Lincolnshire, treating them both as her sons, and friends. She told me that she used to work very hard to maintain the household and pay all bills, whilst her friends were pursuing artistic inclinations, practising music, playing piano, painting and composing. Lydia was very fond of music, and played piano as well, so she found in music another common ground to share with her two friends. But in the end, these two men ended up stealing from her and disappearing with her money and possessions.

Few years after this, when she came to therapy, Lydia told me that she had finally found meaning and purpose in life.

She had started to study Buddhist philosophy and became a dedicated student, enrolling on a long-term course and travelling to specialised retreats.

She bought a house in a village near London and was planning to live peacefully practising the Daoist teachings.

She told me that she practised towards being a truly compassionate individual, accepting of others and all their faults, and loving unconditionally.

After settling in her new place, she had met a man on a dating website and she seemed to care about him.

She said that this man used to come and see her for sex, disappearing for days and weeks afterwards. One day he came to visit Lydia accompanied by another woman, who turned out to be a date from the website. This woman turned aggressive towards

Lydia as she had imagined that this man had no other women in his life.

However, Lydia accepted a relationship with both of them, a ménage à trois, which the other woman struggled with.

Lydia's inclination towards being with couples made me ask her lots of questions about her parents and childhood. I was thinking that, somehow, she needed to recreate something lost, something that would involve both her parents.

Her parents had a very strained relationship; Lydia always suspected that her mother had been abused by an elder uncle; Lydia was remembering times when her parents' violent arguments ended in her mother threatening to kill herself, and even a time when her mother attempted to slit her wrists in the bathroom.

One day Lydia came to therapy and told me that she had found the secret to a perfect relationship. Inspired by her studies in Buddhist teachings, she said that she would never demand anything from a partner, that she would allow him to be able to come and go as he pleases, see other women, and even bring women back to her house.

She resolved to accept all, to never express jealousy or possessiveness, and to 'share him' with other women.

Consciously, she said, she felt 'true and total compassion, selfless love and the relinquishing of a selfish Ego.'

As her therapist, I was not sure if the way she decided to manage her life and relationships was her own phantasy, or she was borrowing other people's phantasies. Philosophy teaches us that our worst nightmare is to be trapped in another's phantasy.

In the subsequent discussions with Lydia, we stumbled across a dream of hers where she was intervening between her parents during a violent fight, in order to separate them. As a little girl, she was hoping that she could stop her parents from fighting, separate them, and thus save her mother's life.

In our talks, Lydia understood that her attraction to couples was not about a desire to be with them; instead it related to her unconscious desire to destroy their bond and separate the couple so as to free them.

When living with others, she was constantly trying to break them apart, and sooner or later, they were becoming somehow aware of her intrusion.

Her phantasy involved not only love, but also hatred and destruction.

Following our work, she resolved to never be near others who already had other partners in their lives; she decided to try and build something with solely one person, and eventually she came to understand that negating her own self was not a sign of love.

The most controversial psychoanalytical concept, *Death Drive* (*Todestrieb*) was discussed by Sigmund Freud towards the end of his life.

Todestrieb refers to a human drive aimed at destroying the self or the other, or to a forceful compulsion to repeat, to fail, to try to return to a state of primordial stasis.

In psychoanalytic theory, *Death Drive* is seen as a vital force that appears to revolve around the objects of our desire, without actually reaching or obtaining them; this very failure or monotony seems to 'satisfy' the drive force.

Perhaps we act according to our *Death Drive* often in our life. We seem to be drawn to something but when we get close to it we renounce it, or we do something to jeopardize our obtaining it.

Our *Death Drive* would be 'satisfied' with this very renunciation or failure.

But if we go closer to the object of our desire, the risk of failure is increased, and also the risk of suffering. I am wondering if in this way (renunciation) we don't actually try to avoid failing and suffering.

And how can we know that getting what we want is not in fact the expression of *Death Drive*?

Because often, getting what we desire, means the end of desire, death of desire, and disappointment.

Also, Desire as opposed to 'need 'or 'wish' is often latent, unconscious.

In reality we may have little idea about what we desire.

But desire will re-surface perhaps in psychoanalytical endeavours, and also in an overwhelming enjoyment of a situation.

In a therapy session some time ago, while talking to a patient who had experienced childhood trauma, and mentioning death drive with regard to our mind repeating painful memories, she asked: 'But what is to be done, what can we do to control our death drive?'

I thought it was a beautiful question whose answer is impossibility.

But I believe that our best chance is awareness.

Awareness of the powers in us, of the things we do in the same way, of persisting with situations that make us suffer, or make others suffer. Our 'compulsion to repeat' is a good indicator that our *Death Drive* may be at work. How many times in life we re-enact the same scenario, with different persons, and sometimes even with the same person? Perhaps we unconsciously hope to obtain a different outcome, perhaps we need the re-enactment itself in order to derive some strange satisfaction from it.

We may be greatly helped by this awareness of repetition and the awareness of the times when we seem to be strangely content when failing to 'obtain' something or someone we want.

XX. SIMPLE THINGS

Some words, here, now, will have to be withheld.

From *Journal of a Melancholic*, unpublished

Anna, aged fifty-four, suffered with depression for most of her life.

In her childhood, as the eldest daughter in her family, she had to look after her siblings and became the main support for her depressed mother after their father left.

In her twenties, she nursed her mother through terminal illness and worked in a care home.

She married at twenty-seven; it was an abusive marriage that lasted for twenty-five years, and she cared for her husband before he died of cancer. Her two sons left for college and then never returned to live at home. Anna lived for the times they came to visit, but these times were rare enough.

The family had moved to South-East London because of her husband's work, though Anna was originally from Glasgow.

Her feelings of melancholia became more overwhelming as a rare event happened to her.

As her house needed lots of repair, she had sought the help of an electrician to fix the old wiring. This electrician turned out to be a handsome young man, and Anna fell in love with him.

She told me that it was the first and only time in her life when she was in love with a man. She only could make tea for him and have short discussions with him. Nothing more had happened between her and the young electrician and she never saw him again after the electrical work was completed.

In therapy she talked often of feeling lonely and useless. I was thinking that all her life had been spent caring for others and that she had to now look after herself, and I told her so.

She was considering selling her large cold house to move back to Scotland where she still had some family left. One of her sons was working in Edinburgh, the other one was living and working abroad in Germany. They would have preferred if their mother stayed in London. She was really afraid of making a bad decision about selling the house, as she was afraid of making any decision at all. I had no idea whatsoever what was best for her, so I tried to mainly listen and encourage her to look at all possibilities. She did seem quite isolated in Greenwich, where she lived, and her neighbours were not known to her.

At the end of our work together (twenty sessions as strictly allotted by the NHS protocol) I reluctantly asked Anna if she had got anything at all from our discussions. She said 'Yes, two important things. I am going to sell the house and return to Scotland. But also, since I started to come here I bought a wool blanket like this one you keep on the sofa. I have got a soft blanket for myself, which I keep on my knees when I read and watch TV – and it feels warm and settled'.

Indeed, when I had started working in that dark but beautiful building belonging to Maudsley Mental Health Hospital, I brought to the therapy room a soft wool throw from home and a banker's desk lamp, in an attempt to make the austere room more welcoming, but I never gave them a second thought.

Anna's decision to sell her house and move to Scotland frightened me a little, but I was content about what she said about feeling less cold and lonely in her home. The wool blanket was a small simple thing, but a sign that she perhaps was getting better at looking after herself.

This was a lesson to me, to never assume that someone who has learnt so much from life already knows and uses simple small things that could make a difference.

XXI. ON PATIENCE

Someone came to my house on this cold day,
To fix a broken thing.
And I did not offer them tea.
And I did not stop them to talk to them.
How sad it must be,
To be someone
That people do not wish to keep,
Even for a moment.

From *Journal of a Melancholic*, unpublished

Most of my patients say from our first discussions and throughout therapy that they want to change who they are, that they want to be someone else.

That they want to get rid of anxiety, of depression, of phobias.

My thought is always that they need strength and fortitude to put up with suffering, and bear with it at least for a while. I am not talking about being abused. That is not something to bear or put up with.

I am talking about emotional states that are not the most peaceful. Emotional states that are tormenting, full of uncertainty, of doubt; that are sometimes unbearable.

In chaos, agony and suffering, there can be important, vital meaning that we are going to discard, and lose, because we are determined to get rid of everything that does not get along with our (sometimes borrowed from others) idea of happiness. And sometimes chaos can lead to beauty and touch perfection, though we might need the help of someone else for this.

For all of my patients, like Anna, I wish I were able to make them tea, maybe in a beautiful old teapot, taking my time.

In all my years of NHS work, I was amazed by the kind habit of my colleagues to make tea for others. It was something I could never offer to do myself, as I felt I would have probably taken a long time. I feel that tea is something that has to be done at our own pace.

The Book of Tea, published in 1906, reminds us of the Taoist story that tries to explain the mystery of love. At the beginning of the great No-beginning, Spirit and Matter were enemies in a fierce and violent confrontation; at last, the Sun of Heaven defeated the lord of darkness and earth, but in his death agony, the dark lord struck and shattered the dome of the sky, throwing the stars and moon into chaos. The Sun of Heaven sought someone to repair the sky and found in the Eastern Sea a divine queen, 'horn-crowned and dragon tailed' who promised to weld and fix the vault of heaven. The queen kept her promise, but she forgot to weld two crevices of the sky. This was the beginning of love, and its dualism, as two souls are destined to never rest until they meet to fill those remaining gaps and complete the Universe.

Sometimes, in therapy, when we understand something really important about ourselves, for a thousandth of a second we dwell in the gaps of the Universe, and our souls find some rest.

XXII. ON SLEEP

What do we understand about insomnia and longing? My blood is not my own anymore, it is someone else's.

From *Journal of a Melancholic*, unpublished

One of my patients, Ralph S., at the age of twenty-eight had already become the head teacher at the school he had taught at for the last five years. He taught German language and literature.

Ralph came to therapy for problems with anxiety and insomnia.

He expected that we would have cognitive behavioural therapy discussions, in which I would also present relaxation strategies.

But these were problems with sleep, so from the first discussion I asked Ralph what sort of dreams he had.

He very reluctantly told me about a recurrent dream in which, stranded on a boat in the middle of a storm, he killed his brother.

Ralph did not return to therapy afterwards.

Sometimes, the real in life, the real in dreams, is difficult to confront. To the point that we would rather be awake than immersing ourselves in this real.

The real can also be our own aggression, rivalry, love force, destructive instincts. In our day-to-day life we might have the choice of kindness, sublimation, therapy.

In dreams though, our power is less our own, we are often at the mercy of the dream.

Another patient, John R., forty-eight, came to see me because of chronic problems with insomnia.

John would tell me about endless nights spent pacing in his bedroom, or going up and down the stairs, or spending time in the kitchen during the night, not able to sleep, no matter how tiring his days were.

He told me that his insomnia problems, tiredness and irascibility had eventually led to the breakdown of his marriage a few years before. A long habit of drug use may have been involved as well.

'It was not the drugs in themselves that I was after,' he said. It had been the 'buzz', the tension of going to get drugs; finding them, purchasing them, seemed to have mattered to him more than actually taking the drugs.

A luxurious lifestyle of holidays and expensive cars had been altered by the end of his marriage as his wife got to keep the one-million-pound family home as well as most of their savings, which left him with loads of debt.

John said that he made a fortune in the real estate domain; as a skilled surveyor by trade, he knew how to find the right property to buy and re-sell. He had used his skill to buy old houses, fix them, and re-sell them within the next six months.

He had started the business with money obtained from remortgaging his first flat that his mother had helped buying.

When we started therapy, he was two years into legal proceedings, trying to recover part of the money that his wife had kept after separation.

He was now living with his mother in her house in Woodford, and he was often travelling across the country for survey assignments as he was now working for a large building corporation.

During his work trips, he would stay at various hotels, where nights were spent awake. He would get less than two hours of sleep during the daytime, in the afternoon. His best nights would bring about two or three hours of sleep, but best nights were very rare. He had given up drugs and alcohol completely.

A few months into therapy, John came to our session smiling gently, stating that he had a good spell where he managed to sleep through the night for a few nights in a row.

When I asked him about any previous events which may have provoked the change, he told me about a surveying job in North Yorkshire where he had to inspect an old building which functioned as a care home for the elderly.

He said that he wandered into a quiet wing, where there were some open doors, and he entered a room where an old man had died that morning and was still on his bed. He watched the dead man lying on his bed; 'He looked so peaceful and kind,' John said.

John said that he had stood there in the room, by the bed, quiet and transfixed, for about twenty minutes, before he was found by the care home staff.

He said that he had no warning about that room, there were no signs on the ajar door, but he had been left on his own to look at the inside of the building as this was his second work visit and staff already recognised him.

When I asked him about any memories that came to life whilst he was standing in the room of the dead man, he told me about his father's death, when John was still a child. When his father died, John was not allowed to see him, and was not allowed to attend the funeral.

He had been prevented by his mother and his aunt, who believed that it would have been too distressing to a young child.

John felt that he had betrayed his father by not being near him in the hospital and by not attending the funeral.

His problems with insomnia and anxiety started around the time of his father's death.

And for some reason, standing in that quiet room with a dead man that reminded him of his father, acted as some sort of protective, redemptive event, and had helped him get a better night's sleep for the first time in almost forty years.

Possibly, when we sleep, we are immersed in the Real. The Real is that which we cannot see, we cannot know, and we cannot bear.

We construct dreams to protect ourselves from the Real. Our tendency to create illusions continues to manifest itself in dreams as well, in a desperate attempt to make sense of the Real, to veil it, to explain it.

We are living illusion after illusion.

When we fail to veil the Real any longer, the Real appears again and again through a tear in phantasy.

We cannot fix that tearing when it occurs and that can be traumatic.

Perhaps tearings give us the mystical ecstasy as well.

It is the same with Psychosis.

The Tear in the Real has to be repaired and that is why *delusions* and *hallucinations* appear. These are another kind of *illusions*.

This time, the attempted fix for the Tear comes not from within, to the Real, but from the Real to Within.

Real – Real in us

Between Real to Real, there is a screen of Imaginary and Symbolic.

We are caught up in this Screen, between The Real in us and the Real outside us, where us is our consciousness.

Real – Imaginary, Symbolic, Ego – Real

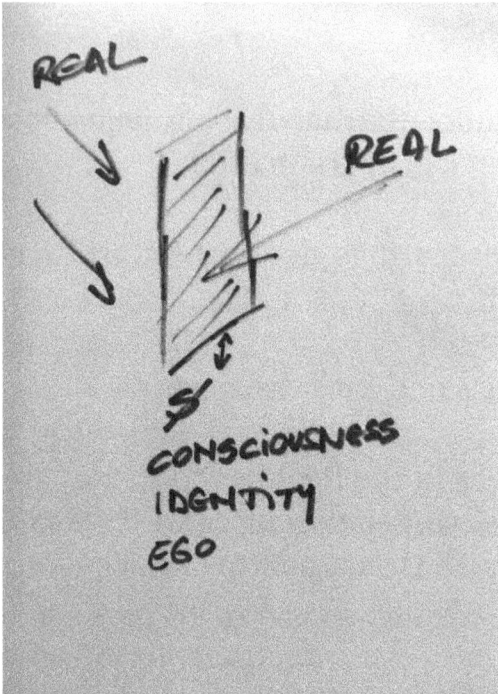

The Real in us versus the Real outside Us.

The Unconscious is part of the Real in us.

There is the Real outside us.

In the Screen, we fabricate thoughts, ideas, religion, hope.

XXIII. TRAUMA

I understand more about fracture and losing everything. I have been an orphan since then. Nothing could fill, replace, caress. I wonder if I had not sought the emptiness as well.

The emptiness in me, the emptiness around me. It's not nothingness, it's something else.

What role did fate play? Did I create my own fate? My own curse? My own solitude?

From *Journal of a Melancholic*, unpublished

Four years ago I saw a Polish female patient who had been through some traumatic events: caught in a terrorist attack whilst on holiday in Tunisia, then a serious fire at their house. She was referred by her GP for Post-traumatic stress symptoms and anxiety.

During our discussions I came to believe that the need to talk about these recent events hid another need, a need to talk about something else that may have been really traumatic, so I asked her directly.

My patient Maria was in her early twenties. With great difficulty she said that she had been abused by the father of her childhood friend when she was four or five years old.

She realised that this had happened only later on in life, when she was fourteen. The meaning of what had happened was constructed afterwards, when she became a teenager and she had left her native town and country.

I have found in therapy that, sometimes, those who lived traumatic experiences talk about something else frightening because they are not able to talk about the event that is really painful and that stayed with them for a long while.

Maria told me that she could not possibly talk to anyone else about the abusive neighbour, as her family would have certainly 'sought revenge'.

It was the first time she could bring herself to tell someone what had happened.

I remember that rainy day, with her crying in the old leather armchair, I did not know what to say or do, more than to hold her and let her cry on my shoulder.

Later on, we made detailed plans regarding contacting the Police in her native town. She resolved to tell her family what had happened.

In psychoanalysis, traumatic memories about childhood events bring to attention the concept of *Nachträglichkeit* or *afterwardsness*.

Afterwardness, retroaction, après-coup, is a concept that defines our attributing a certain meaning to a past experience only at a later time in life.

For Maria, the later experience of becoming a stranger, a foreigner in another country, enabled the construction of the memory of the childhood abuse.

Indeed, meaning is often constructed retroactively and this is not true only of early sexual experiences, but it is relevant to many life experiences.

Something happens in life where we had felt a certain way when we lived through the event; but looking back on it, with new information at hand, we may give it an altogether different interpretation and we may feel differently about it. Meaning is not set in stone.

More than one meaning is in fact possible related to one single event.

Someone meets a new person, and what seems to be a regular encounter, may come to mean a lot to this person's life. Maybe an important friendship, maybe someone who inflicts suffering or someone who teaches something important, nevertheless, the meaning of the encounter is often established retrospectively.

We get to understand more about our destiny, retrospectively.

Psychoanalytic theory highlights that traumatic encounters represent brushes with the Real. Somehow, witnessing and suffering from the extent of evil in some humans is considered in psychoanalysis to be, the Real.

Most interactions between people will function based on desire and demand. But if love does not dwell in these, it is for the best that such interactions do not happen.

I believe that we need to change our over-rating of humans. Not all charged interactions with other humans, evil or good, are Real events. Only intersections with Fate constitute Real events.

We live in times when paying back for a wound inflicted on us by others might be considered revenge. It might be useful to keep in mind though that the Old Testament prescribes, 'Burning for burning, wound for wound, bruise for bruise' (Exodus 21:25).

XXIV. DESIRE FOR DESIRE

The force of wanting you demolished and changed me forever but it did not move one atom in the universe.

From *Journal of a Melancholic*, unpublished

Desire is no easy domain to deal with.

One of my patients, a beautiful Mathematics teacher in her late thirties, told me that while dating a much older man with whom she had no physical contact, she was dismayed to find herself having sexual phantasies about his twenty-seven-year-old son.

She and her date went to visit his son for a couple of days in Oslo where he was doing a PhD in Physics. The Maths teacher found a lot to talk about with the young scientist, but she also felt it had been more than just a professional interest that they shared.

This may not be such an out of the ordinary phantasy, but there was more to it.

Not only did the young handsome son appear intrusively in her thoughts, but also his father appeared as a spectator of these phantasmatic encounters, as a third man present, watching, seeing inside the sexual phantasies.

The motif of another, of a third element, of the figure of the father made us talk about her own relationship with her father for many sessions afterwards.

We continued working together exploring questions related to desire, and what it meant to desire. She decided though to stop seeing the friend that was older than her and where desire was lacking.

How can we understand what happens when we strongly desire someone?

Where does the overwhelming desire come from? What are we supposed to do with desire? Resist it? Follow it?

Is desire the same as love? Whilst there must be some overlap between desire and love, still, desire is not love.

When we are desired, we are not necessarily loved. When we desire, we may not love at all.

To desire someone or something is to foresee that we will feel joy or happiness in their or its nearness. That we will feel joy or happiness even in the absence of words. The desiring itself gives us joy.

We can get lots of pleasure just by looking at something. Our eyes, often, lead straight to our heart.

How can we prevent ourselves from looking at something or someone? If we watch someone and we feel desire, we have a choice. There is the option to look away or to go towards them.

If we linger in our look, if we look again, if we advance into nearness, we have already made some choice to follow our desire.

A moment of desire, if and when we are free-to-desire, can be something to cherish. It is something that brings our heart into a dream, a phantasy.

A moment of desire is not free of suffering either. It is perhaps a memory of something lost, or the awareness that we cannot have something we want.

Not always in life it is true that, 'where there is a will there is a way.'

There are things, and people in life, that we shall never be close to, even if the sky was to fall.

I do not mean that this is what we should seek, pursue, moments of joy. In our quest for life and permanence, these moments seem to nonetheless come into our life.

The sadness of our times though is that we are often mistaking happiness for satisfaction or comfort.

We cannot deny that real joy and happiness are entangled with chance, some sort of providence, but also with struggle, courage, and faithfulness.

XXV. ON PARANOID THINKING

Stars that we don't see but we guess they are there. Forests over stars, all light only comes from the eyes of the passers-by.

I have lost my way and I cannot find it again. The world is full of words and the darkness is split into syllables.

Madness is God's punishment. And perhaps so is love. Punishment for a great trespassing. But whom, and when, have we trespassed against?

From *Journal of a Melancholic*, unpublished

On an April afternoon, Samuel, thirty-three years, came to the session wearing an old wool jumper with holes in it. It still looked like a very beautiful jumper, probably knitted by hand; I did not ask by whom and I regretted not asking.

I remarked that he was late for the session.

He told me that he had met a woman from a dating website for casual sex.

He said that she arrived at his place in the afternoon, they slept together, she then left and he made his way on his bike to the Steel's Lane Health Centre, in Commercial Road, a forever busy road in the East End of London.

'And how did the encounter make you feel?' I asked him.

'Empty', was his reply.

Samuel's most ardent wish was to become well known, to become famous through his work. As an artist, a painter and illustrator, he hoped that one day his paintings would bring him fame.

His childhood had been in an idyllic place in the Wiltshire countryside, with very strict parents, especially his father who was a pastor at the local church.

When Samuel was thirteen and his sister eleven, there had been an incident where he came across his sister undressed. This was an obsessive memory and he talked about it often in therapy, blaming himself, feeling guilty and ashamed for seeing her, and for 'her shame'.

In his youth, he was troubled by his sexuality, stating that his encounters with women did not make him feel what he was 'hoping to feel'.

In his famous psychoanalytic work *The Case of Schreber*, Sigmund Freud attempts to interpret a case of madness, a case of delusional paranoia, based on the autobiographical material of the subject, the judge Daniel Schreber. This is one of the most important cases of psychoanalysis, as it provided the foundation for further developing the psychoanalytic theory of paranoid illness and psychosis.

Sigmund Freud constructs the mechanisms of paranoia based on the negation and repression of homosexual desires. He stated that in some paranoid people, homosexual wishes are repressed, negated and inversed, so the idea 'I love him' will become 'I hate him' (I hate him because he persecutes me, delusion of persecution).

Also in paranoid people negation can become: 'It is not I who loves Him, but it is She who loves him' (delusions of jealousy), 'I do not love Him, I love Her' (in eroto-mania, where a man seems to engage in many love affairs), 'I do not love anyone, I only love myself' (in megalomania).

Sigmund Freud teaches that, in paranoia, the delusions of persecution will culminate into wishful phantasies.

In Schreber's case, the wishful phantasies revolve around his becoming (such as) a woman, surrendering to the love of God (both in a physical and spiritual way), being in the presence of God, creating new people, facing the power of the Sun.

Sigmund Freud states that the repressed homosexual wishes that are at play in paranoia have been, in childhood, directed at the father and brothers, and that in 'normal' men they are at the basis of male friendships.

While working as an illustrator in a large publishing house in London, Samuel used to have delusional fears that others could read his thoughts – these others were his managers and colleagues. He thought that they could know that something was amiss with him, that he was 'marked by shame', that he was someone 'mad'. He thought that they looked at him in a peculiar way and that often they talked and whispered about him.

After months of agonizing with his paranoid suspicions and quite convinced that everyone in the office was now part of the conspiracy, he left his job that he had worked very hard to secure.

We started therapy soon after his quitting work.

His most important goal remained, to become well known and famous as an artist.

His days of intense creative work would be entangled with daydreaming of the time when he would be famous: he could see his paintings on the walls of art galleries; crowds of people would look at them and marvel. He would then be allowed to live a different lifestyle, one of luxurious but intimate parties. He would describe these parties to me sometimes: there were extremely handsome young men and women attending, dressed in fine clothes and wearing exquisite fabrics and jewellery; there would be classic music and vintage turntables, exquisite cocktails, and always the place would resemble the rooms of a stately home.

It was possible that Samuel's paranoid thoughts were indeed sutured with wishful phantasies: the fear of being known as 'mad', as 'marked by shame' with the phantasy of being well known through his work that he considered different, touched by genius.

His problems at work could have been indeed close to a delusion of persecution by others, but linked to a wishful phantasy: to be known and loved by the Other.

XXVI. THE BODY

The love for you mixes with the Love for Him,
and it is so that I am eternally lost in this fire
flow of love.

From *Journal of a Melancholic*, unpublished

My psychotic patient Avraham, forty-two-year-old, had started telling me about succubi and incubi from our very first discussion. He started with a tentative sentence, looking at me intently, as to check whether I thought he was crazy.

But in general I think that everyone, including me, is somewhat crazy, and I knew almost nothing about succubi and incubi. I listened with interest, and probably nothing in my attitude discouraged him, as he proceeded to explain.

He told me that, apparently, incubi are lustful demons who can visit women at night for the purpose of possessing them and having sexual intercourse with them. The female form of these demons is called succubi.

Avraham believed that he was made into some sort of Incubus by the gods.

I asked him what made him believe so. He told me that, few times in his life he was attracted to very beautiful women, that seemed 'out of reach' and somehow, he was allowed to hold them and to be with them, as if by miracle.

He told me about being attracted to a beautiful neighbour of his who invited him over to her house one evening.

'I am being made into an incubus, so I can be with her. As an incubus, I could have any woman I desire, but I only want to be with her'.

Demons are eternal, and all powerful, and my patient had created this delusion in his mind, in which he could be the same, eternal, and all-powerful. In this delusional phantasy however, the human trait of faithfulness remained.

If there was, let's accept just for one moment, a time before the original sin, what would have desire been like for Adam and Eve?

Or should we say desire in Adam and Lilith? Lilith was Adam's first wife, made not from rib but from clay, the same as Adam. The story of Lilith is obscure, and it is unclear why she departed the Garden of Eden, whether she was a *demoness*, or whether she was involved with the fallen angel Samael.

Were Adam or Eve ruled by desire?

Was it desire to know? Was it desire for happiness, desire for purity? Desire for God? Desire for suffering?

The not-knowing meant that they did not know about sex either. Until they learnt. The serpent interferes and functions as an Other, the symbolic order. Would they have known, without the interference of the serpent?

Would children know about sex, without the interference of adults?

Obviously, children know pleasure. Pleasure of eating, touching, warmth. But what does this mean? Does it follow that these senses have to be engaged just because they can lead to physical pleasure?

The problem of orgasm is relevant here. Why was this physical pleasure made possible for humans?

What was the purpose of it?

Of course, we should not relate sex and masturbation to physical pleasure alone, as often they are driven by anxiety, loneliness, fear.

But why are we also able to know that there are higher pleasures, higher ecstasies?

In psychoanalysis, we talk about feminine *enjoyment*, feminine *Jouissance*, feminine *Passion*.

Feminine Passion is pleasure that does not necessarily have to do with sex and physical pleasure. It is ecstasy that goes beyond the sexual function. It is often akin to the union with something sublime, supernal (even in some situations when close to humans).

To return to the question of body – for massage therapists, it is well known that there are areas of the body that offer extreme relaxation and pleasure when touched and massaged. Yet, somehow this is not used, not encouraged on a large scale, does not seem profitable. Profitable to whom?

We have to ask, why should everything about humans be used and made profitable?

Can we not accept that there are areas that are charged, and can bring extreme pleasure, and still, not be used?

We always have the choice of trying to find alternative charged areas, more lofty, more permanent.

If men are able to only enjoy mostly in a limited way, through their own bodies, they will not be able to understand what is happening for women, who can enjoy in almost ecstatic ways, largely closed out to men. The union between men and women is asymmetric and fractured because of this.

I cannot really give any advice to women, but still, I shall try: try to not sleep with someone you do not wish to marry. If you do not want them in that way, it means that you do not want them enough, it means that they do not want you enough.

Try and decide if the traditional way of physical intercourse is what you want. There are lots of opinions that there is not enough satisfaction in it for women, and that lots of women do it just to please men. If it is not what you want, simply, don't do it.

Women can decide to live, as women, without fulfilling their sexual function, without being embodied by the sexual.

There is the possibility that the sexual was not created just to be necessarily used. We do not have to use every function that has been given to us in a way which mostly we have learnt how to use. A way which we have learnt from others.

XXVII. OBJECT CAUSE OF DESIRE

Short-lived immanence. I have lost you before I have ever had you.

From *Journal of a Melancholic*, unpublished

Laura was a tomboy. My patient with beautiful blue eyes, thirty-eight, always wore trainers and jeans, had short hair, and worked as a sports journalist, writing for several big newspapers.

She used to come and see me after long walks in Maida Vale. Walks, she said, greatly helped with her anxiety.

She had a very difficult relationship with her mother and her two sisters. Laura talked a lot in therapy about her sisters, especially the middle one who had tried to commit suicide twice.

Laura had been her father's favourite, always accompanying him on fishing trips and to sport games. Her father was a businessman and a writer who had written a rather successful detective novel. He seemed to be very loved and adored by the whole family. Laura described him as the centre of the family.

She was often talking about how much she learned about sports from her father.

She was often wondering, and asking in sessions why her sisters were always so competitive and unloving towards her.

One day I asked her if she could imagine how painful it must have been for her sisters to witness that she was the preferred child.

She thought about this for a while and she became tearful. She said: 'It must have been heart-breaking..'

We have already touched in the book upon *Objet petit a*, the indicator of desire, that which we want in someone or something, that which attracts us, but often fails to keep us. An *elusive mark* which cannot be explained. This elusive mark is at the basis of desire, and as such is the cause of desire. This takes us back to the idea of primordial loss, losing someone, or something.

The cause of our desire is not supposed to be a fallen object, a thing.

What we have lost, what we are forever searching for in life, is something beyond material, something to do with love, warmth, acceptance.

Of course there will be something in others to remind us of what was lost, perhaps the colour of their eyes, the way they look at us, the sound of their voice, a gesture, or certain words they use.

This does not mean however that the lost 'object', and the cause of desire is the same with a physical trait. Perhaps that is why we are never satisfied with what we have; we can never really find what we are looking for, because what we want goes beyond a feature, beyond things, beyond words.

In his Seminar on *Transference,* Jacques Lacan discusses the theme of *agalma*: some

DR LIA T. ASANDEI

elusive precious object that is hidden in the 'hideous' depths of someone we desire or love. Here, the precious object seems to be related to knowledge, to knowing. Highlighting the idea that knowledge is also bound to love.

Let's highlight again, that there is a difference between love and desire. Desire is desire and, love is love.

Let us not forget though that Jacques Lacan's influential psychoanalytic ideas of *agalma and transference* are based on the exegesis of an old ancient text, Plato's *Symposium*. The love and desire that are reflected in the *agalma*, related to Socrates, Alcibiades and Agathon, are mostly types of love based on a specific (homosexual) love.

It would appear unfair then to apply the concept of *agalma* to *all situations of transference and love.*

The *elusive mark* is of the Real, the impossible, and the divine.

XXVIII. SECRETS

The recollection of unbearable moments that cannot be told in words. Yet I remember them, and how it felt. Is it possible that our memories have nothing to do with words then? How do we store feelings?

What happens with affect in the unconscious? How does this relate to the Other?

From *Journal of a Melancholic*, unpublished

We try so faithfully to find answers and anchors in psychoanalysis, science, the Bible, philosophy, novels, poetry, dreams.

There are some partial answers in there perhaps, there are some real answers perhaps but how can we really know?

When all is said and done, all has been written and created by people. Even though these people are 'enlightened' or wise, or even people who have experienced visions, how can we really know, how can they really know?

In observing people, it does seem that some possess 'luck', and things go well for them, and the others are unfortunate. These very concepts, 'luck', 'fate', 'destiny', 'existence' have been created by people, they stem from people's beliefs.

Even though there might be a divine Providence to which even gods submit.

One is deemed 'lucky' or 'unlucky' by the standard of collective human phantasy. Someone very wealthy or famous may be thought of as quite lucky, and if we hear that someone wealthy or famous committed suicide, we attribute this to depression, and not to unhappiness. After all, someone famous and wealthy cannot be unhappy, people believe, they must be somewhat mentally disturbed if they are not satisfied with their life.

Happiness can be measured in intensity. There are kinds of happiness that seem to trespass into madness. Perhaps people are only allotted a certain amount of happiness. Perhaps some people will have lived such happiness in a short time, that they will have exhausted all other possible happiness onwards.

There are people who live unbearably happy times and lives, and yet, they are not wealthy, nor famous, nor known. They are just anonymous people whom we will never hear about.

There are also many anonymous people who keep their agony hidden and manage somehow to go through life. Sometimes in therapy we learn about them.

A patient told me that for most of his life, his father had a habit of gathering newspaper clippings with all sorts of extraordinary facts from around the world. These curious facts mainly related to lost animals and things that somehow found their way back to their original owners.

This was a time from before the Internet, and his father would keep a drawer in a cupboard of his room, full of clippings and photos from various newspapers. When family members were visiting, his father would take some articles out and read them aloud. And this happened despite the family insisting that, instead, he should tell them about his own life experiences, such as living through a war.

My patient's father had been a soldier in the Second World War and had fought on the Eastern front. His first wife had died in the war, leaving him with a small baby boy; two years after losing his wife he remarried. This first son was not to survive, he had died at the age of five, from a fall when left unsupervised. Another son (my patient) was born from the second marriage.

My patient often talked about a deep sense of sadness at losing his half-brother when he himself was still very small. His questions about his brother remained unanswered by his parents and he often found himself terrified by thoughts that his own mother could have been negligent, or worse, towards this brother.

And still, the stories my patient's father chose to tell later in life were not his own stories, but random stories of people that he did not know. Stories about something lost that was found again, and loved again.

His own story was the one that he could not, or did not wish to tell. Collecting newspapers' stories was his 'thing', his way of 'keeping it together', but also a way of keeping a veil over his own secret.

In the same way, most of us have our own way of keeping life together, a way of keeping our own veiled secrets, which we may not even be aware of.

XXIX. ON WORDS AND MAGIC

You dared me to fall
Into words
What fall can still be there
When I am at the limit
Of all words.

From *Journal of a Melancholic*, unpublished

In Psychoanalytic theory, Sigmund Freud asserts that, in the beginning, words and magic were the same thing, and that today, words have still retained something of the primordial magic.

Even though our position within language is very limited, we can still try and find words that are different from the everyday meaning. We can try and find words and ways of expression that say something deeply personal, in a very personal way.

We can try and say something to others that they may not hear all the time. We can try and find a name for those we love that is not being used by lots of people, for other people.

We can try to be absolutely honest in ways that people, for the sake of polite conversation, have forgotten about or have never known. Full honesty does not need to be vulgar or harmful to others, indeed, it can be really endearing.

We can try and find the magic that was lost in words.

I am trained in Freudian and Lacanian psychoanalytic theory, which would tell us that, 'a person's jealousy is pathological' even in a situation when there are clear signs that their partner is being unfaithful.

But then, if you study The Zohar, you might come across the idea that, 'there is no true love without jealousy.' And to read this in a book written a thousand years ago it lends the idea more heaviness.

I am writing this chapter in April 2020, when people around the world are under lockdown because of a virus epidemic.

As human contact is limited, often communication with others happens only in words, written or said over the phone or the Internet.

When we cannot touch people in reality, we can try to touch them in words. We can employ the magic in words and turn them into spells.

The old book of Zohar will remind us that, '*said* does not mean spoken by mouth, but it is rather the silent wish of the heart.'

XXX. ON DEATH

To live amongst stars and to get confused in the inversal between sky and earth.

From *Journal of a Melancholic*, unpublished

Matthew M. came to see me after he was diagnosed with pancreatic cancer, few years prior.

I learnt that he was a professional violin player, a virtuoso, who had made his musical debut at Wigmore Hall in London in the eighties. His life had been of music, but in a space of ten years he became increasingly disappointed by the calculative life that music concerts demanded.

He withdrew more and more from the musical world and in his early thirties he eventually left London and moved to Jerusalem.

When he came to see me, he was visiting London to see his brother and to undergo medical tests for his illness.

I asked him how he spent his time since his estrangement from the concerts world.

Matthew told me that he continued to play and perfect his music but his only audience was, now, his own family, his children and wife, and sometimes, some close friends and neighbours.

He was also spending more time with philosophical and religious texts.

As a therapist, I was in awe of Matthew. How many people would give up a successful musical career? How many would recognize that we do not live only for others, that we do not have a duty towards them?

Matthew's father died from cancer when Matthew was very young, and he grew up with his mother and his brother. His mother, a famous musician herself, was very strict and imposed severe rules about education and music practice; Matthew had started to play violin from a very early age.

Although of Jewish roots, he was brought up a Catholic, and Judaism was rejected in the family home. Matthew and his brother were not allowed to keep in touch with other Jewish family members, or to have friendships with other Jewish children. Religious books were not allowed in the house, and holy days were not observed.

Matthew's parents moved to England from Germany after the Second World War, and Matthew told me that his grandparents had been deeply observant of religious life; one of his great grandfathers was a passionate scholar of the Torah and The Talmud, who would worship in a beautiful, small local synagogue.

I was thinking that Matthew chose a path of his own desire and love, by keeping music in his life only for him and his loved ones and by studying the holy books. Psychoanalysis teaches us that what is repressed often finds a way of returning in our life.

I felt very free to speak to Matthew as we only had a couple of discussions during his time in London.

I asked him whether his life was happy and he answered: 'I think I have found a happy life; I always felt that I would not have long to live.'

I thought to myself that Matthew always lived in the awareness of the end.

He died from illness one year after our discussions, at the age of fifty-eight. There was almost no mentioning of his passing away in the media.

As Martin Heidegger reminds us in *Being and Time*, we are 'Beings-towards-death'.

The thought of death is, nevertheless, in our social life, mostly concealed and even kept from us.

We live amongst others and they have a way of protecting us from thinking about death.

We say 'one dies', and through this we distance ourselves from this truth, we flee in the face of it.

But philosophy reminds us that awareness of our finitude brings freedom.

To me, awareness of the end is about the courage of acting, knowing that we cannot spend all our time hesitating.

It is about deciding how to spend our life, when we are more aware that it is not endless.

It is about not allowing others to hurt us; we do not have the time to waste on being mistreated.

If we were more aware of death, we might choose to spend our life differently.

We might decide that we do not have all the time to put up with situations we cannot change, with people we cannot change.

We might decide that we do not wish to put up with some people and situations at all.

Or, on the contrary, we will make a decision to dedicate our life to something, to someone.

However, such awareness of finitude does not come only with freedom, it also comes with fear, anxiety, sorrow, regret.

While the ideas of death may be in the *Symbolic* and *Imaginary* realm, I see death and finitude as belonging to the Real, to Das Ding, to the Thing, to the transcendental, to the core of us.

The same Real that we screen and veil in phantasy.

It is just that, sometimes, phantasy fails and the Real is revealed to us, even if not in its entirety and certainty, even in just a glimpse.

Before the psychoanalytic Real, there is a primordial Real.

The primordial Real, The Thing, Das Ding that is in us and around us.

In the absence of Faith, we all try to reach the Thing through Art, Science, Music, other people, work, wealth.

We try and try and often fail.

The Thing is veiled in beauty and it inspires terror.

Perhaps that is why we are attracted by Beauty, and thrilled by Terror. We play with the Thing, we go near it, and we withdraw.

It fascinates us and it frightens us.

The thing in us calls us, calls the Thing. The Thing calls itself.

Whatever we believe we know about death, and any fears that we may have about it, these are beliefs that are mostly learnt.

We are not able to understand how death and happiness fall into each other. Happiness occurs in being near the Thing, approaching it.

We get to touch sometimes the Thing that owns us and this gives us beatitude.

Love, in all its different shapes, not only erotic, has often been associated with The Thing, perhaps because of the impossibility to explain love, to account for it. And we shall be fallen objects, things, unless we are (like) the Thing.

XXXI. WOMEN

What is the value of a dream if it is dreamt by all? I cannot take refuge but in my own dream, that belongs to only You.

Faith is a story of unrequited love.

From *Journal of a Melancholic*, unpublished

Sarah M., thirty-eight, was a beautiful single mother of two beautiful boys, and a construction executive working full-time.

She and her husband separated after eleven years of marriage, after she was told by another woman, through Facebook messages, that her husband was meeting other women through dating websites.

There had been bouts of disbelief, arguments, reconciliations, and then a definitive rupture.

When Sarah came to therapy one year after the separation and her ex-husband moving out from the family home, she told me that she was not dwelling so much on the breakup, and she, 'did not feel heartbroken any longer'. On some days she was cheerful, but on later days she started to talk about her anxiety and sadness. I was relieved when she could talk about anxiety, sadness and tiredness, I felt that she was allowing herself to feel like this, that she was allowing herself to mourn.

She used to come to our therapy sessions late in the evening after a long day at work.

She would have some limited support with raising the children from her parents and ex-husband, but she did almost everything by herself.

She was working full-time, looking after the boys, trying to help her ill parents as well as friends, as she said, she was, 'trying to get on with life'.

She would often talk about underlying anxiety, but most often, feelings of guilt would surface.

Especially on a day when her younger son fell ill at school, she felt guilty for not being there for him, for not being able to leave work straight away in order to be with him.

There was guilt for, 'not recognising what was going on in her marriage,' guilt for 'not being good enough, not a good enough mother, not a good enough wife, not a good enough daughter'. It had been terribly difficult for her to let her parents know about the end of her marriage.

As a therapist I used to be dismayed by these feelings of guilt in someone who was trying so hard, who was giving so much to others.

When we ended working together, Sarah thanked me also in writing, assuring me that she had taken a lot from our discussions. She was trying perhaps to make sure that she was not, 'a not good enough' patient.

But is this not a problem that we all face?

Being constantly demanded of, fulfilling duties and roles, loving, being sometimes betrayed, betraying others, we come to think that we are the only ones at fault. That we are not good enough, that we do not give enough, that we do not do enough, that we are not enough.

So often we forget that the other is (also) guilty, that others are, at fault.

Women, feminine women, seem more open to be influenced, to be moulded. Moulded by families, friends, lovers. We can be suspicious of women's strength of character.

I look at the jobs women do. They often do hard, impossible jobs. Nursing, for example. It is a job that can be most difficult and it involves lots of tasks that squeamish people would not be able to do: for example, to draw blood. However, lots of women do these nursing jobs. Are women tougher, less squeamish? Are they more empathetic or more caring? Are they more susceptible to take orders?

Women are all too conscious, and unconscious of their sexual function and procreation role. What if this was to be annulled for them? Would women still exist?

Would they still continue to exist if they were, no more and no less, than men's companions and equals?

If they were to be immersed in whatever else: dance, books, poetry, walking, cooking, dreaming, working, writing, painting, swimming, all sports, philosophy, astronomy, spells etc.

But then, who would look after the human species and assure its continuity?

I have no idea. The human race will have to figure that out for itself.

Why should the duty to continue the human race fall on me, or on you?

This is indeed an extreme view, I know.

But there are gentler ways.

Love has thousands of ways in which it can be expressed.

If you love or desire someone, you can listen to them, really listen to them, spend time with them, cook for them (if you enjoy cooking), hold their hand, hug them, get them the most interesting gift that you can afford, understand them, be silent with them. And nothing more.

XXXII. MEN AND WOMEN, UNITE

My soul is so tired; it cannot even bear the heaviness of seeing your eyes.

To hold your hand would simply kill me.

From *Journal of a Melancholic*, unpublished

In 2018, when working at the Whittington NHS Trust, I saw Hannah A., thirty-six-year-old, who was referred to therapy for difficulties with anxiety and depression.

A single mum, Hannah lived in Hampstead in her mother's flat with her four-year-old son Damien. Her ex-partner would help with looking after Damien at weekends.

Hannah often talked about her difficult relationship with her mother.

She spoke of her mum's struggle with depression, her absences from reality and problems with memory. Hannah would sometimes trust her mother to look after Damien, but would constantly worry about this, especially as Damien had some health problems.

She was happier to bring Damien along to our discussions, and let him watch documentaries about dinosaurs and owls while we talked.

When leaving the consulting room, Damien would be curious and look into other office rooms with glass doors and run along the corridors, apparently disturbing my managers who would tell me off about seeing patients who brought their children along to therapy sessions.

One day Hannah told me that she was glad she had a son and not a daughter.

'I would not have been able to love a daughter,' she said.

When I asked her more about this, she gave it some thought and then said, 'I would have wanted what she had. I would have been jealous of her'.

I tried to understand more about the statement that a daughter would not have been as loved. I asked Hannah whether she felt unloved by her mother. Hannah said that her mother's life as a single mother had been very difficult but she did not give up on raising her, although she seemed to have struggled with depression. Her father, a successful surgeon, had left them after Hannah was born. Her mother used to work long shifts at the hospital as a nurse, and take Hannah along to work, so as, 'to not leave her with strangers'. Hannah would play and draw in a small room at the hospital, which was both a changing room and a storage area for medical supplies.

Still, the relationship with her mother was always fraught and Hannah was somehow saying that she found it impossible to find the love between her and her mother.

On that November rainy afternoon, at the end of the talk when she mentioned not wanting a daughter, as she was putting her coat on, after she helped Damien with his coat, Hannah said: 'I am going to stop and buy some cinnamon buns for my mom. I never get her anything, and she really likes cinnamon buns'.

Psychoanalysts and psychologists have this habit of trying to find the cause of everything. Philosophers talk about 'absolute recoil' where the effects of a cause can create their cause retrospectively.

But there are times in our life when we can actually feel tired with trying to find the cause of something.

The reality of the effects is important and clear enough.

If we feel that we are not loved, why should we try so hard to find out why?

If we cannot love, is it so important to ask why we cannot love?

Hannah felt that she was not loved by her mother, and she felt she could not love a daughter.

I remembered another patient who said once about becoming a mother: 'When we came back from hospital, my baby girl used to look at me as though she was reproaching me for the fact that I did not want her. Indeed, I wanted a son instead'. She said this with a guilty, painful smile.

I often wonder why men appear to need less love that women do.

But sometimes it appears to me that I do not have to know what lead to this. Even the Bible teaches that men have been allowed to divorce their wives, because their 'heart is hard', but that it was not like this from the beginning (the Gospel According to Matthew). Was there a time when men's heart was not hard? When was this other beginning?

We need a new beginning.

The greatest taboo of Psychoanalysis is not that men cannot love, but that women are less loved, in general, even by other women, even by their own mothers. No wonder that later on in life they will put up with situations where they are not loved enough, and they will continue to hope for love. Perhaps all feminist struggle and all the suffrage is indeed women's plea to be as loved as men are.

As more time goes by, and more books are written, the divide between men and women is deeper and more decisive.

In the ancient world of Greece, men's love was mostly love for young boys. The adoration of handsome boys may have taken many forms, including platonic love, but also some sort of sexual touching. There is another idea surviving, that sexual touching or intercourse was shameful to the boy; nevertheless, the boys were able later on in life to carry on marrying or having intercourse with women.

When did this way of loving change?

Has the love for boys been repressed?

Have Judaism and Christianity changed things? In what way?

Psychoanalysis seems to say that men are more inclined to hate than to love women. And there are even feminist ideas that men are not able to love.

I find in my work with patients that men's love for women belongs to the impossible, or the divine.

Psychoanalysis talks about masculine women though, and feminine men. It talks about obsessional women and hysterical men as exceptions.

Psychoanalysis keeps repeating that *The Sexual Relationship Does Not Exist* ('Il n'y a pas de rapport sexuel'). What we often see between two people is a non-relationship. This is to say that a 'sexual relationship' is not really a relationship, this is to say that a 'physical relationship' does not necessarily bring two people together.

Psychoanalysis (Jacques Lacan) also asserts that, 'Woman does not exist'. If Woman does not exist, what is this being that we call woman then? Perhaps women are trees.

Can women not be beautiful trees?

If Woman does not exist, then she can be anything. A dream, a phantasy, a poem, a story.

I believe that women are not purely women, and men not purely men. Feminine and masculine elements can exist in a woman, the same as in a man, in different proportions.

I came to believe that whilst a 'sexual relationship' cannot guarantee a real bond between a man and a woman, a common interest, or goal, could. Men and women who seek to transform themselves through a passion for a certain domain of creation or skill have better chances at sharing their lives.

Sexuation may exist in us innately, but I cannot help but observe that it is 'transmitted' to us as well. Adults transmit to children, both consciously and unconsciously, a message regarding sexuality. The conscious message is easier to spot: for example, many schools organise sex education lessons. How is children's age determined for starting 'sex education'? Why is this necessary so early in life? All these are matters decided by adults.

Films and TV shows that are meant and made for children, will inevitably contain scenes that will make children know things, wonder and ask questions.

Children always seem to come across scenes that do not make sense for them, that are curious or disturbing to them.

And most importantly, children are surrounded by and immersed in words, with their various and ambivalent meaning.

I am not sure why 'sex' or 'sexual relationships' have to happen. What is the point of them? Physical pleasure? Intimacy? Do 'sexual relationships' lead to intimacy?

Why cannot sex be reduced only to those who love or believe that they are in love?

And banned to all the rest.

REFERENCES

Friedrich Wilhelm Nietzsche, *Beyond Good and Evil (Jenseits von Gut und Böse. Zur Genealogie der Moral)*, New York, The Modern Library, 1919

Alain Badiou, *In Praise of Love,* London, Serpent's Tail, 2012

Bruce Fink, *Lacan on Love: An Exploration of Lacan's Seminar VIII, Transference*, Cambridge, Polity Press, 2015

Jacques Lacan, *The Seminar of Jacques Lacan, Freud's Papers on Technique, Book I, 1953-1954*, New York, W.W. Norton & Company, 1997

Jacques Lacan, *The Seminar of Jacques Lacan: The Ethics of Psychoanalysis, Book VII, 1959-1960*, New York, W.W. Norton & Company, 1992

Jacques Lacan, *Transference, The Seminar of Jacques Lacan, Book VIII*, Cambridge, Polity Press, 2015

Jacques Lacan, *The Sinthome – The Seminar of Jacques Lacan, Book XXIII*, Cambridge, Polity Press, 2016

Martin Heidegger, *Being and Time,* New York, Harper and Row, 1962

Okakura Kakuzo, *The Book of Tea,* London, Penguin Classics, 2016

Plato, *Complete Works,* Indianapolis, Indiana, Hackett Publishing Co, Inc, 1997

Paul Verhaeghe, *On Being Normal and Other Disorders: A Manual for Clinical Psychodiagnostics,* New York, Routledge, 2018

Rob Weatherill, *The Sovereignty of Death,* London, Rebus Press, 1998

Rollo May, *Man's Search for Himself,* New York, W.W. Norton & Company, 1953

Rollo May, *Freedom and Destiny,* New York, W.W. Norton & Company, 1982

Sigmund Freud, *The Standard Edition of The Complete Psychological Works of Sigmund Freud,* London, The Hogarth Press, 1964

Søren Kierkegaard, *Either/Or,* Vol. I, New York, Anchor Books, 1959

www.ingramcontent.com/pod-product-compliance
Lightning Source LLC
Chambersburg PA
CBHW050230270326
41914CB00033BA/1859/J